DISCOVERY IN FILM, BOOK TWO

DISCOVERY IN FILM BOOK TWO

Malcolm W. Gordon

Designed by Emil Antonucci

PAULIST PRESS
New York/Paramus, N.J.

Library of Congress
Catalog Card Number: 72–92734

ISBN: 0–8091–9526–7

Published by Paulist Press
Editorial Office: 1865 Broadway, New York, N.Y. 10023
Business Office: 400 Sette Drive, Paramus, N.J. 07652

Printed and bound in the
United States of America

Acknowledgments

Communication Theme Break, from "A Letter to Alceu Amorosa Lima;" *White Society from* "Introductory Notes to a White Liberal;" *Loving God*, in SEEDS OF DESTRUCTION by Thomas Merton. Copyright © 1961, 1962, 1963, 1964 by the Abbey of Gethsemani. Reprinted by permission of Farrar, Straus & Giroux, Inc.

Divisions, Dealing Fairly with Others by Eric Hoffer in the New York Times Magazine, April 25, 1971. Copyright © 1971 by the New York Times Company. Reprinted by permission.

The New Morality by Rollo May in the New York Times Magazine, March 28, 1971. Copyright © 1971 by the New York Times Company. Reprinted by permission.

Hippies at the Stock Exchange, Money: The Green Fetish from DO IT! by Jerry Rubin. Copyright 1970 by Social Education Foundation. Reprinted by permission of Simon & Schuster, Inc.

Alienation from THE POLITICS OF EXPERIENCE by R. D. Laing. Copyright © 1967 by R. D. Laing. Reprinted by permission of Penguin Books Ltd.

Developing a Spiritual Life from THE RELIGIOUS SPEECHES OF GEORGE BERNARD SHAW. Copyright by the Public Trustee of the Estate of George Bernard Shaw. Reprinted by permission of Pennsylvania State University Press.

Eternity and Time, The Writer from THE CREATIVE EXPERIENCE by Stanley Rosner and Lawrence E. Abt. Copyright © 1970 by S. Rosner & L. E. Abt. All rights reserved. Reprinted by permission of Grossman Publishers.

A Word about Tonto from CUSTER DIED FOR YOUR SINS by Vine Deloria, Jr. Copyright © 1969 by Vine Deloria, Jr. Reprinted by permission of The Macmillan Company.

Do not go gentle into that good night, THE POEMS OF DYLAN THOMAS. Copyright 1952 by Dylan Thomas. Reprinted by permission of New Directions Publishing Corporation.

A Teen-Age Nader Raider Reports from "The Story of a Teen-Age Nader Raider" by Bernard Law Collier in the New York Times Magazine, March 14, 1971. Copyright © 1971 by the New York Times Company. Reprinted by permission.

Film and Objectivity from an interview with Federico Fellini by Gideon Bachmann from a forthcoming volume to be published by Simon & Schuster, Inc. Reprinted by permission of the author.

The Price of Hating, Effects of the War from NO BARS TO MANHOOD by Daniel Berrigan, S.J. Reprinted by permission of Doubleday & Co., Inc.

The Native from "Fanon: The Revolutionary as Prophet" by Horace

vii

To Joseph A. Slattery, S.J.

"And gladly wolde he lerne and gladly teche."

Geoffrey Chaucer
The Prologue
The Canterbury Tales

CONTENTS

Introduction

Discovery in Film Book Two is meant as an introduction and a guide to the booming field of 16 millimeter short films. The 16 mm. film, long regarded as an amateur's field, has come into its own in recent years. In both the number of films produced and the number of first rate artists working in the field the 16 mm. film has outstripped the rest of the field.

This book aims for both quality and variety in the films it treats. It does not pretend to be exhaustive but attempts to be as comprehensive as possible in touching the major areas and styles of 16 mm. films now being produced. There are photojournalistic films, the NBC documentaries are good examples here, which emphasize the presentation of current social issues. There are also what have come to be known as anthropological films, which attempt to document the many and varied life styles and cultures of humanity that can be found everywhere from New Guinea to West Texas. *Dead Birds* and *Blues Accordin' to Lightnin' Hopkins* come to mind in this context. Animation of an adult variety primarily springing from Eastern Europe, experimental cinema from New York City, and exercises in visual imagination from California also are styles of film making that are reviewed here.

The point of the book is to provide easy access to a number of excellent films in this growing field. Since some may not be suited to a particular audience, every attempt is made to describe as carefully as possible the style and content of each film.

One final note. For every film included in this book roughly two were rejected. There are still a lot of bad films around which are still listed in catalogs. I have found that one of the best guides to films is word of mouth. Anyone interested in film, especially for use in the classroom, should try to keep in contact with others who are doing the same thing. This multiplication of eyes and ears will save much time and hopefully prevent the disastrous experience of the boring film.

Addresses
Film Distribution Centers

1 Association Films, Inc.
25358 Cypress Avenue
Hayward, California 94544

2221 South Olive Street
Los Angeles, California 90007

8615 Directors Row
Dallas, Texas 75247

512 Burlington Avenue
LaGrange, Illinois 60525

2nd and Delaware Avenue
Oakmont, Pennsylvania 15139

484 King Street
Boston, Massachusetts 01460

600 Grand Avenue
Ridgefield, New Jersey 07657

5797 New Peachtree Road
Atlanta, Georgia 30340

Association-Industrial Films
333 Adelaide Street West
Toronto, Ontario

2 Brandon Films
34 MacQuesten Parkway South
Mt. Vernon, New York 10550

3 Carousel Films, Inc.
1501 Broadway
New York, New York 10036

4 Center Cinema Cooperative
c/o Columbia College
540 North Lakeshore Drive
Chicago, Illinois 60611

5 Center for Documentary Anthropology
24 Dane Street
Somerville, Massachusetts 02143

6 Contemporary/McGraw-Hill Films
(Eastern Office)
Princeton Road
Hightstown, N.J. 08520

(Midwest Office)
828 Custer Avenue
Evanston, Illinois 60602

(Western Office)
1714 Stockton Street
San Francisco, California 94133

7 Filmakers Cooperative
175 Lexington Avenue
New York, New York 10016

8 Filmakers Library
290 West End Avenue
New York, New York 10023

9 Flower Films
1412A North Poinsettia Place
Hollywood, California 90046

10 Grove Press Film Division (Minimum order: $25.00)
53 East 11th Street
New York, New York 10003

11 Mass Media Ministries
2116 North Charles Street
Baltimore, Maryland 21218

1720 Chouteau Avenue
St. Louis, Missouri 63103

12 NBC Educational Enterprises
Room 1040
30 Rockefeller Plaza
New York, New York 10020

13 New York University Film Library
26 Washington Place
New York, New York 10003

14 Paulist Productions
17575 Pacific Coast Highway
Pacific Palisades, California 90272

15 Polymorph Films
331 Newbury Street
Boston, Massachusetts 02115

16 Pyramid Films
Box 1048
Santa Monica, California 90406

17 ROA's Films
1696 North Astor Street
Milwaukee, Wisconsin 53202

COMMUNICATION

Everything healthy, everything certain, everything holy: if we can find such things, they all need to be emphasized and articulated. For this it is necessary that there be genuine and deep communication between the hearts and minds of men, communication and not the noise of slogans or the repetition of cliches. Genuine communication is becoming more and more difficult, and when speech is in danger of perishing or being perverted in the amplified noise of beasts, perhaps it becomes obligatory for a monk to try to speak.
Thomas Merton

OH WOODSTOCK

In one sense this film is a stunt. Two separate groups of people react to identical news footage from the Woodstock Rock Festival. We see first five young people who had been to the festival view the film and give their reactions to what they see. Then five older people view the same footage and react to it. This stunt, or psychological experiment, if you will, is the heart of the film, and on a small scale, at least, it is highly effective.

Oh Woodstock can be said to show that a lack of communication between people is not simply a matter of different words but of different languages. The young people's comments are typical of their milieu. Their reactions to the film they see reflect a deep sense of their common values, values that are more than a collection of words. They reach back to and reflect to a common psychological reservoir of fears and aspirations that are typical of their age.

The same comment can be made of the older people who view the film. In their case, especially, it is not so much what they say but how they say it. Their reactions range from almost total outrage to fumbling attempts at understanding. There are fears and aspirations expressed here too.

Oh Woodstock is a highly concentrated form of communication. As such it is a two way street. It tells us something about the film maker and the people in the film.

6

More importantly, perhaps, how we react to it tells us something about ourselves. We too have our reservoirs of fears and aspirations. *Oh Woodstock* can help us clarify what that reservoir consists of.

26 minutes—color
Rental—$15.00 (#12)
Purchase—$330.00 (#12)

Suggestions for the Use of
OH WOODSTOCK

1: If possible, repeat the experiment that is the basis of the film. Show the footage of *Oh Woodstock* to a group of teenagers and then to their parents or to an older group. Try to get their separate reactions. Tape record them, if possible. Then show the whole film to the whole group, and get their reactions.

2: The question of how people communicate is just as important as what they say. Are the people in the film calm and relaxed as they respond to the scenes at Woodstock or are they upset and angry? If they are upset, what reasons do they give for their frame of mind? Is it possible from the tone of voice that each person uses to express his reaction to surmise what that person's value system might be?

A possible point to be made here is that we communicate with each other on many more levels than just words. What we say is often less important than how we say it. And how we say something almost invariably points to the center of our personhood.

DIVISIONS
How many and deep are the divisions between human beings! Not only are there divisions between races, nations, classes and religions, but also an almost total incomprehension between the sexes, the old and the young, the sick and the healthy. There would be no society if living together depended upon understanding each other.
Eric Hoffer

THE NEW MORALITY
The old morality was essentially a superego morality. I don't think the new emerging morality will have much to do

7

with the superego . . . Now we are getting an organismic human being who feels his way into the standards he is going to live by.
Rollo May

SALES TRAINING: JAPANESE STYLE

Here is another study in communication. At first viewing it appears funny, almost ridiculous. The full impact of what is going on only dawns on us later. For five minutes we are given an inside look at an intensive training program for Japanese salesmen. The program is a non-stop marathon session designed to train men to sell. It is not just the surface of the salesman that the session is supposed to reach but the whole person. Everything from strenuous physical exercise to psychological indoctrination is employed to transform the eager aspirant to a high-powered seller.

The violence in the film is not even thinly disguised. You sell successfully by literally wearing the customer down to exhaustion. To the victor belong the spoils.

16 minutes—color
Rental—$3.45 (#12)
Purchase—$65.00 (#12)

Suggestions for the Use of
SALES TRAINING: JAPANESE STYLE

1: Project the film without the title and the sound-track. Have the viewers guess what the film is all about.

2: Are there any parallels to be drawn between "free enterprise" and karate, or is the program shown in the film totally silly and impractical?

HIPPIES AT THE STOCK EXCHANGE

The Stock Exchange official looks worried. He says to us, "You can't see the Stock Exchange."
We're aghast. "Why not?" we ask.
"Because you're hippies and you've come to demonstrate."

"Hippies?" Abbie shouts, outraged at the very
suggestion. "We're Jews and we've come to see the stock market."

vision: *The next day's headlines:*
NEW YORK STOCK MARKET BARS JEWS

We've thrown the official a verbal karate punch. He
relents.
The stock market comes to a complete standstill at
our entrance at the top of the balcony. The thousands of brokers
stop playing Monopoly and applaud us. What a crazy sight for
them—longhaired hippies staring down at them.
We throw dollar bills over the ledge. Floating cur-
rency fills the air. Like wild animals, the stockbrokers climb all
over each other to grab the money.
"This is what it's all about, real live money!!! Real
dollar bills! People are starving in Biafra" we shout.
We introduce a little reality into their fantasy lives.
Jerry Rubin

THE BREAK

This is a short and terrifying film. A young couple
ride home early in the morning on a New York subway. They sit
apart and do not speak. We sense that something has occurred
that has damaged their relationship. They leave the train and start
home through a large abandoned lot. On their way through the
lot they are attacked by a group of derelicts. This sequence is so
shot and put together that it suggests an almost surreal quality
to the physical action it portrays.

Then the attack is over. The couple more psychologically than physically harmed reach out wordlessly for each
other as the film ends. The film can be said to be symbolic in the
sense that it is much more than a simple portrayal of a physical
attack. The isolation of the couple and the impersonality of the
derelicts suggest a scene from a medieval morality play illus-
trating the faceless evils that surround us in our daily lives. The
derelicts can be taken as simple muggers while at the same time
representing the interior forces of despair and loneliness which
we find deep within ourselves.

11 minutes—B&W
Rental—$8.50 (#13)
Purchase—$80.00 (#13)

Suggestions for the Use of
THE BREAK

1. *The Break* is a student film, and the film maker is trying to convey something more than just a straight narrative. He is carefully using the capabilities of the film medium to create the effects he desires. For example, what evidence does he give us about the relationship of the couple at the beginning of the film? How does he position his actors? What kind of lighting does he use? How does he use his camera, i.e., why does he use long shots and shots photographed from various angles? How is sound used in the film?

ALIENATION

We are born into a world where alienation awaits us. We are potentially men, but are in an alienated state, and this state is not simply a natural system. Alienation as our present destiny is achieved only by outrageous violence perpetrated by human beings on human beings.
R. D. Laing

THE POKER GAME

The framework of this dramatization is a weekly poker game that is usually attended by the same six men, all old friends. They know each other and feel comfortable in each other's presence. The one particular night with which the film deals a stranger tags along, ostensibly just for a hand in the game. The development of the drama revolves around this stranger who inter-acts with the six men and gets to a level of communication with them that is strange to them. Where before they had been hiding from themselves by empty activity, now in the presence of this stranger they almost are forced to open themselves more and more. The comfortable facades they had projected themselves and accepted in the others become less and less acceptable.

As the night progresses the men are forced to become more honest, a process which isn't necessarily the most com-fortable experience one could hope for. Their reactions to this experience expressed by their actions toward each other and to the new member of the poker game provide the climax of the

film's dramatic interest. The fears and anxieties of men forced
to face themselves hold our interest to the conclusion of the film.

28 minutes
Rental—$17.95 color (#1)
       11.95 B&W (#1)
Purchase—$270.00 color (#14)
       135.00 B&W (#14)

Suggestions for the Use of
THE POKER GAME

1: The film is really about the compromises we make
with ourselves in order to face the world and our own selves
more comfortably. A character by character analysis of the film
would make an interesting and informative discussion. What
makes each one of them tick? What is the conflict in each one of
the men? What problems in their lives are they trying to come to

grips with, or avoid? What role does the new member of the game play in the drama? How does he affect the action of the drama?

2: This film would make a good companion piece for *Oh Woodstock!* The same questions of role playing in our lives are touched upon in both films but developed in a different way. A comparison of how the two films address themselves to their similar subject matters would be most profitable.

COMPUT-HER BABY

"Computers never lie about love." *Comput-Her Baby* is a visual parody on the notion of computer dating. The film is slick and jazzy rather than profound, and it relies heavily on trick photography and sophisticated laboratory techniques to get its point across. Although it deals primarily with the absurdity of the use of computers to bring people together, it also can be used to start a discussion on a wider point, viz., the dehumanizing effects of machines on our modern lives.

4½ minutes—color
Rental—$10.00 (#16)
Purchase—$75.00 (#16)

Suggestions for the Use of
COMPUT-HER BABY

1: A film like *Comput-Her Baby* can be ideally used in a multi-media situation. With another more serious film on the main screen and a series of slides and *Comput-Her Baby* on two secondary screens an effective light collage can be presented.

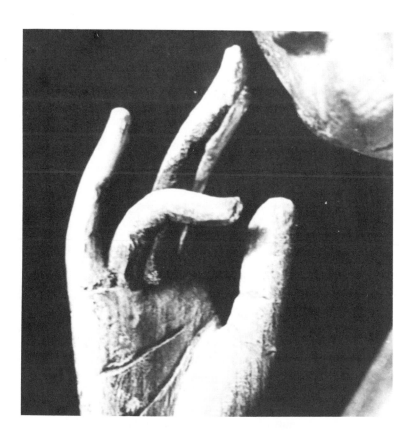

AWARENESS

Awareness is a simply beautiful film. It was made by the same man who made *The Parable,* Rolf Forsberg. Where *The Parable* tended to be a bit too literal and simplistic for my taste, *Awareness* shows that Forsberg has developed into a film maker with a sensitive and imaginative control of the medium.

The film is an attempt to convey the subtle truths of the Buddhist approach to life. It succeeds eminently in its difficult task of expressing visually essentially non-visual attitudes and concepts. The film opens with a brief reenactment of the experience of the young Buddha as he leaves his sheltered home for the harsh outside world. Forsberg himself narrates this passage closely following the Buddhist scripture. After this opening narrative passage there is a careful intertwining of visual and verbal imagery as we follow the development of the consciousness of the young Buddha to his final awareness.

The final passage of the film is a sensitive documentation of the Japanese Tea Ceremony and the explanation of the world view behind the ceremony that is sensitive and unforgettable. This whole last scene is put together with an economy and perceptivity that quietly brings the viewer into a whole new way of looking at life. *Awareness, Survival with Style,* and *Blues Accordin' To Lightnin' Hopkins* are the three best films in this book.

22 minutes—color
Rental—$25.00 (#11)
Purchase—$300.00 (#11)

Suggestions for the Use of
AWARENESS

1: This film deserves to be seen twice. A good idea might be to show the film first without any introduction then have the audience discuss or write what it was about and what they thought of the film and why. Then show the film a second time and see if any new reactions have been evoked.

2: Play a section of the film's soundtrack and have the audience suggest visuals that might go along with the soundtrack they have heard.

3: Is this film an attempt at a logical argument for an intellectual point of view or is it an attempt at what its title suggests, a new awareness? More importantly what is the difference?

LOVING GOD

The way I would express it now, is in purely religious and symbolic terms. That we should "love God" not merely to convince ourselves that we are good people, or to get a warm glow of peace, or to fit in with an approving group, or to get rid of anxiety, but to throw all that to the winds, and anxiety or not,

14

even though we realize that this simply does not matter in the "eyes of God" for, as we are, with our misfortunes and needs, "we are His joy" and He delights to be loved by us with perfect confidence in Him because He is love itself. This is of course not capable of being put in scientific language, it is religious symbol, or if you prefer, "myth."
Thomas Merton

DEVELOPING A SPIRITUAL LIFE
There is no hope for us in economic socialism or in anything else unless we develop our spiritual life. If we do not it will be a very bad thing for this country; it will be a very bad thing for us; it will mean the wreck of another civilization.
George Bernard Shaw

FRIENDLY GAME

This is a subtle and disturbing film. Its power lies in its quiet ability to unsettle our rather smug view of ourselves and what we really feel about other people. The film is really a cleverly disguised confrontation between basically conflicting values that we thought we had covered over with a pleasant covering of civilized politeness.

The setting of *Friendly Game* is a rather posh chess club. A white man sartorially correct with a personality to match invites a black man whom he takes to be a new member to a friendly game of chess. The friendly patter of the white man fits in perfectly with the urbane atmosphere of the club. He is secure and comfortable in his own milieu and exudes the sophisticated confidence of a man who has mastered the rules of the game. The game here, of course, is not just chess but rather the totality of civilized rules that everyone accepts as to how life should be lived.

The black man is also well dressed but quieter and more reserved. He seems to accept his role as a novice willing to be educated in how the game should be played. The initial mood, then, is one of quiet equilibrium. The white man knowledgeable and confident in the rules of the game is gently initiating the black novice in the proper subtleties of making the proper moves.

As the game progresses, we realize that there is much more going on here than a simple game of chess. The game starts quietly enough, and the black man begins to lose. Then, suddenly, he challenges the white man to a bet, one hundred dollars versus the chess set. The surface pleasantries evaporate as the two go at the game in deadly earnest. The communication between the two becomes more real as the artificial layers of civility which cover the gross hatreds of our society are stripped away. In less than ten minutes we have gone from the correct atmosphere of the club to a primordial struggle which is played for keeps.

10 minutes—B&W
Rental—$15.00 (#11)
Purchase—$135.00 (#11)

Suggestions for the Use of
FRIENDLY GAME

1: This is a carefully made film with the director able to carefully select his settings and direct the precise movements of his actors. It would be a profitable exercise in film criticism to analyze each element in the film such as speech, dress, physical position and physical movement of the actors and see how each contributes to the film maker's purpose.

2: What is the role of manners and courtesy in our

society and in our lives? Why do elements in our society make a point of violating "good manners"?

WHITE SOCIETY

Why, in this particular crisis (and this applies to international politics as well as to domestic or economic upheaval), is there so much hatred and so dreadful a need for expressive violence? Because of the impotency and the frustration of a society that sees itself involved in difficulties which, though this may not consciously be admitted, promise to be insuperable. Actually, there is no reason why they should be insuperable, but as long as white society persists in clinging to its present condition and to its own image of itself as the only acceptable reality, then the problem will remain without reasonable solution, and there will inevitably be violence.
Thomas Merton

DEALING FAIRLY WITH OTHERS

The fundamental indifference toward us of most of the people we meet is a fact we are extremely reluctant to accept. Yet it should serve as a basis for our fair dealing with others: we must expect little, and we must give people some sort of vested interest in us to rouse and hold their interest.
Eric Hoffer

IN THE KITCHEN

In the Kitchen is a unique little piece of cinematic art. In the film the camera set in the corner of a small room that serves as kitchen and bedroom for a small, working class Yugoslav family never moves. From this fixed viewpoint we see two mini dramas unfold concurrently on the screen. The first deals with the humdrum but rather affectionate and happy life of the family we see in the kitchen; the second portrays an incident in the more active and passionate loves of the two young people we see on the balcony across the courtyard from the kitchen.

The strength of the film is not based on the cinematic trick of the fixed camera, but rather on the subtle power of suggestion that the film employs. In a sense we learn very little about the people in both the situations we see developing. In a wider sense, though, we see and learn a great deal. The family quietly eats lunch and prepares for an afternoon nap. Their

17

actions are perfectly normal and routine, but they are also carefully choreographed to express the most delicate nuances of their affectionate relationship.

In the background on the balcony opposite their window the couple quarrel, separate and bring their relationship to a different ending. The irony in the film is the fact that their physical closeness to the family in the foreground means little in the light of their vast psychological distance.

12 minutes—B&W
Rental—$15.00 (#11)
Purchase—$150.00 (#11)

Suggestions for the Use of
IN THE KITCHEN

1: This film demonstrates what is known as a busy screen. There is a lot of simultaneous and significant action occurring in each frame of the film. How does the film maker contrast the simultaneous activities of the two groups of people? What actions occur at the same time that are contrasted?

2: The film is ideal for a basis of a discussion on the isolation we experience in our modern cities.

ETERNITY AND TIME
Eternity is a bore, you know, when you don't look at it through the

window of time . . .'To get those two together, I think that's really the essence of craftsmanship.
Arthur Koestler

BETWEEN TWO RIVERS

Communication is a problem between people. It can also be a problem between cultures as this film painfully illustrates. This NBC documentary focuses on the story of James Hawk, a Sioux Indian, who is now serving a life sentence for the violent crimes of murder and rape. The film is in no way a muckraking sensation seeking thriller. It is rather a sympathetic and sensitive analysis of the hidden undercurrents in an Indian's life that may have led to James Hawk's tragedy.

We review James Hawk's life which in many ways is typical of today's American Indian. We see the people with whom he lived and feel the painful crisis of identity that they are going through. One way to come to grips with their lives is to try and make it in the white man's world, a situation they didn't ask for but are forced to accept.

James Hawk was in many ways a typical bright young Indian. He had been born and raised a Sioux but had decided to make the leap to the alien culture that surrounded him

19

and his people. All the film tells us directly is that he didn't make it. He was a student at the University of South Dakota when he suddenly went beserk and for all practical purposes destroyed himself.

Between Two Rivers never really goes into what went wrong specifically with James Hawk. Instead it simply explores the environment that he grew up in. It is a world where parents know that their children have the highest mortality rate in the country and where the average life expectancy is 44 years. It is a hard life but in many ways a comfortable one and not an easy one to leave. James Hawk really couldn't.

The film is really an introductory statement, to the depths of the problem of the Indian in America rather than a detailed analysis. It succeeds admirably, however, in what it sets out to do. The suffering of James Hawk is an experience we are not able to easily shrug off.

26 minutes—color
Rental—$14.40 (#12)
Purchase—$330.00 (#12)

Suggestions for the Use of
BETWEEN TWO RIVERS

1: As is obvious this film is an excellent basis for the beginning of a consideration of the problem of the American Indian. It presents enough material in itself to form the basis of a discussion, but more importantly, it makes us want to know more after it has made us initially aware.

2: The film can also be the basis for a discussion of guilt. The notion of communal responsibility for the ills of society is a complicated one, but one that is becoming more and more pressing as the world shrinks. The tragedy of James Hawk could be the basis for such discussion.

A WORD ABOUT TONTO

The supreme archetype of the white Indian was born one day in the pulp magazines. This figure would not only dominate the pattern of what Indians had been and would be, but also actually block efforts to bring into focus the crises being suffered by Indian tribes.

It was Tonto—the friendly Indian companion—who

galloped onto the scene, pushing the historical and contemporary Indians into obscurity.

Tonto was everything that the white man wanted the Indian to be. He was a little slower, a little dumber, had much less vocabulary, and rode a darker horse. Somehow Tonto was always there. Like the Negro butler and the Oriental gardener, Tonto represented a silent subservient subspecies of Anglo-Saxon whose duty was to do the bidding of the all-wise white hero.

Tonto cemented in the minds of the American public the cherished falsehood that all Indians were basically the same —friendly and stupid, Indeed, the legend grew, not only were tribes the same, but all Indians could be brought to a state of grace— a reasonable facsimile of the white—by a little understanding.
Vine Deloria, Jr.

ALL WE ARE SAYING

The Washington Peace March of 1969 is now a fact of history. *All We Are Saying* is an attempt to capture the spirit of that event. The beauty of the film is that it does not strive to hit the audience over the head with the sensational highlights of the day, but attempts rather to present the day's events in all their diversity.

The people who made up the huge crowd were not all of one stripe, as the film maker, Al Shands, is able to point out. They were made up of all kinds of individuals of different backgrounds and various persuasions. Shands takes the time to bring us closer to some of these people and present them as sincerely concerned persons rather than as anonymous faces in a crowd. The power of the film does not rely on showing us the huge number of people who showed up to demonstrate their solidarity. In fact from the shots that Shands has chosen to show us in the film we get only a slight idea of how many people were actually there.

In a sense this film is a communication about a communication. The people at the demonstration were saying something most emphatically. Not just the fact that they came to Washington, but what they did and how they presented themselves also said something that cannot be avoided. The film is useful primarily because we see persons not crowds, and we are able to reflect and discuss them as real people.

17 minutes—color
Rental—$20.00 (#11)
Purchase—$200.00 (#11)

Suggestions for the Use of
ALL WE ARE SAYING

1: The most obvious use is to utilize the film as the basis for a discussion of the peace movement in general. There are enough viewpoints in the film that are expressed in words or in actions that would normally evoke a response in an audience.

2: Many different films have been made about the Washington Peace Moratorium, and Al Shands' film is just one of them. As a film maker he has a definite point of view which he expresses by what he chose to shoot and how he juxtaposed or edited these shots in the film. *All We Are Saying* is a good film for analyzing how a documentary film maker presents his point of view by his selection and editing of shots. The film can be broken down into scenes and the impact of each analyzed.

I THINK THEY CALL HIM JOHN

Old age like death is something we are always willing to put off for a while. In a very real sense one of the pains of old age is a slow losing of connections with what we once had, people of our own times who shared our experiences and interests. Slowly the communion with other people becomes more and more infrequent. We are less and less able to keep up with the world physically and psychologically. We are left alone.

I Think They Call Him John records the unpleasant reality of old age with quiet honesty. It shows us a day in the life of a retired miner. He lives alone in a small flat going through the motions of life, a life that has passed him by. In a very simple and undramatic way the film brings us into his consciousness. The dull routine of his daily activity that is almost more of a series of acquired reflexes learned for a life that no longer is and the days that seem to blend indistinguishably into one another are the unrelenting truth of this film.

Many films on old age try to dodge the issue with a touch of gran and gramps sentimentality. Besides being untrue, they are also no help to anyone trying to confront reality. In a

22

world of highly mobile families and a rapidly improving medical technology the aged are becoming a social reality that must be humanely dealt with. *I Think They Call Him John* brings that reality home.

26 minutes—B&W
Rental—$17.50 (#11)
Purchase—$175.00 (#11)

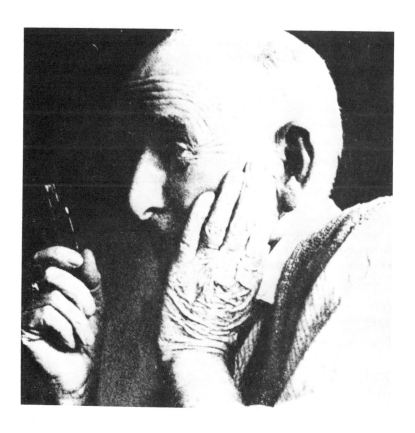

Suggestions for the Use of
I THINK THEY CALL HIM JOHN

1: Most of the documentaries in this book serve as a good basis for a discussion of the topics with which they deal. *I Think They Call Him John* is no exception. The film, though, is not the presentation of a program for the curing of this social problem. It is more of an introduction into an awareness of what it means to be old. There is a danger, I suspect, of attempting to come up with a social program to answer the problems we

see in these films especially the documentaries. Most of the time trying to deepen the awareness of what the film is all about would be more to the point and, in the long run, much more fruitful.

2: Old age is not an intrinsically exciting subject for a film. It is a subject that is naturally resistant to slickness. *I Think They Call Him John* is a good example of how a film keeps our interest in a slow subject. How does the film maker keep the film moving? Why does he arrange the shots that he has chosen the way he has? What does each shot or sequence of shots tell us about the subject?

Do Not Go Gentle into That Good Night

Do not go gentle into that good night,
Old age should burn and rage at close of day;
Rage, rage against the dying of the light.

Though wise men at their end know dark is right,
Because their words had forked no lightning they
Do not go gentle into that good night.

Good men, the last wave by, crying how bright
Their frail reeds might have danced in a green bay
Rage, rage against the dying of the light.

Wild men who caught and sang the sun in flight,
And learn, too late, they grieved it on its way,
Do not go gentle into that good night.

Grave men, near death, who see with blinding sight
Blind eyes could blaze like meteors and be gay,
Rage, rage against the dying of the light.

And you, my father, there on that sad height,
Curse, bless, me now with your fierce tears, I pray.
Do not go gentle into that good night.
Rage, rage against the dying of the light.
Dylan Thomas

June 27

In one home in Virginia there were almost no activities. The patients on warm days were wheeled up to the front porch where they were able to watch the cars rush by on a dirty highway or to overlook the adjacent cemetery. A few watched an unfocused television, while others sat around the nurses' station and stared absently at the opening and shutting of the elevator door.

Janet Keyes' Journal

BANG HEAD, GO BANG, BANG

A question on communication that is becoming more and more prominent in our contemporary society is communication with one's self. Relating to other people is one side of the question, but we must also ask ourselves if we have our own heads together. Do our own inadequacies and self apologies for our own failures twist our views of the outside world? In *Bang Head, Go Bang, Bang* Michael Siporin puts this problem before us in uniquely cinematic terms.

The film examines the mixture of fantasy and reality that filters through the hung-over brain of the hero of the film, a young bar fly, as he attempts to recall the night before through his morning after alcoholic haze. While this can ostensibly be called a narrative film, the story line is actually there to keep your attention while the real guts of the film goes to work on you. Our hero's gropings at recollection are psychologically valid in their confusion yet are mirrored with a precision of cinematic form that is the real beauty of the film.

The structure of the film is basically cyclic. We start with the hero, puffy faced and hung over the morning after a minor binge, sporting a huge headache. We follow him on one false start after another in his quest for truth: how he got that bang on his head. On these involuted trips of introspection we see revealed more and more the private world of his mind, replete with his own peculiar fantasies and frustrations. We shift easily with him from the harsh brightness of reality to the shadow world of his petty egocentricity.

The sense of time that the camera catches sets up a rhythm in the chaos. Again and again we are led visually through the maze of his alcoholic recollections, but the circle is drawn tighter each time. Flashbacks and still photographs, as well as a carefully controlled editing technique that imposes a strict order on the surface chaos, are all employed to bring the film to its final bitter revelation.

The strength of the film is in its exploitation of the resources of cinema. Shot in black and white, it utilizes the film stock fully in recreating the precise pictorial quality that the form of the film demands. We are led flawlessly through the numerous transitions from reality to fantasy with only the slightest hints from what is happening on the screen as to where we are psychologically. *Bang Head, Go Bang, Bang* has a subtlety that grows on you with each viewing.

9 minutes—B&W
Rental—$10.00 (#7, #4, #10)
Purchase—inquire (#7, #4, #10)

Suggestions for the Use of
BANG HEAD, GO BANG, BANG

1: *Bang Head, Go Bang, Bang* is an excellent example of the imaginative use of the techniques of film making. It ideally should be shown more than once. The first viewing should be to simply see what the film is all about. Most likely there will not be total agreement as to what is actually happening in the film. The second viewing should make much clearer what really occurs on the screen and reveal more clearly the techniques the film maker used to achieve his total effect. *Bang Head, Go Bang, Bang* is an excellent film to show as an introduction to

what is loosely called the underground or avant-garde film.

FILM AND OBJECTIVITY

What I am interested in is showing the things behind the things, not just to make statements on what can be seen. I'm often criticized for this—people say that I see reality fantastically deformed. But that is a superficial comment. I think everyone sees life around him in a more-than-superficial manner. What's the sense of being "objective" in film? I don't even think it's physically possible.
Federico Fellini

HIGH LONESOME SOUND

This is a film distributed by Flower Films, a company in California that seems to specialize in beautiful documentaries on the musical culture of America. *High Lonesome Sound,* a film by John Cohen, deals with the music of the hill country of Appalachia. We see the hard life of the coal miner made a bit more bearable by the musical interludes of the likes of Roscoe Holcomb and his music.

This film like *Blues Accordin' to Lightnin' Hopkins* and *Spend It All* successfully captures the integral relationship of a people and their music. It is part of the very fabric of their lives.

The film is a beautiful portrait combining images of sight and sound that seem to flow naturally together.

29 minutes—B&W
Rental—$50.00 (#2)

Suggestions for the Use of
HIGH LONESOME SOUND

1: The film would provide an excellent complement for the NBC documentary, *The Young Uns.* The two films deal with the same people, the Appalachian whites, but from different points of view. When shown in the same series, they should provide the basis for everything from a discussion of their common subject matter to their divergent film styles. What is the point of each of the films? How do the respective film makers go about presenting their material? What shots do they choose

to show us, for how long, and in what order? What use do the two films make of the soundtrack? Does the sound used in each film support the visual image directly or does it provide a contrast?

2: *High Lonesome Sound* is an excellent film to include in a program dealing directly with music. As mentioned in the review Flower Films has an excellent collection of films dealing with the musical culture of America. The only drawback for their use in some situations is their relative expense. Films of such outstanding quality, though, are well worth their cost when shown in a school festival or assembly where their value will become apparent.

CHROMOPHOBIA

Chromophobia is a short allegory on repression. Its title stems from its clever utilization of color imagery to make its point about the repressive pressures that can arise from the simple intolerance of a society. The film is an animated short that tells the story of a small town resplendent in the variety and beauty of its colors that is invaded by a horde of dark, grim soldiers. The relentless soldiers set out to destroy the colors that they find around them and replace them with dull, mundane unattractive blacks and greys.

A series of harsh measures are employed to ensure that the colors are destroyed and that the drabness remains. The citizens of the town are force fed through a gigantic machine that renders them all homogeneously dull, and guards and watch-towers are employed to reinforce the status quo.

The powers of colorlessness appear to have won the day when suddenly they are put to rout by the resurgence of flowers of every variety and color. The townspeople are sparked into a carefree rebellion, which is encouraged by the inability of the soldiers to repress them. The soldiers' weapons fire not bullets, but flowers. Color again reigns supreme.

Chromophobia is included in this section on Communication rather than in the section on Freedom with the hope that it will be more imaginatively used. The film can easily be used in a program devoted to freedom, but its use as an illustration in lack of communication might prove more fruitful. The opposing forces in the film, color and drabness, can be easily seen to have arisen as enemies from an original lack of communication. This antagonism could be analyzed and parallels found for it in our

28

contemporary society. Communication breaks down when there is a basic fear between the communicators that prohibits any exchange of ideas or feelings. The usual result is a savage violence that is both physical and psychological. All these questions can be explored and developed using *Chromophobia* as the starting point for the discussion.

11 minutes—color
Rental—$15.00 (#11)

Suggestions for the Use of
CHROMOPHOBIA

1: What is the effectiveness of the use of color as the central metaphor in the film? What are the connotations of color, for example, what does it mean to say that a person or place is colorful?

2: *Chromophobia* can be used very effectively with films such as *All We Are Saying, Oh Woodstock* and *Reduction*. These three films all deal with a similar theme but from different points of view and film techniques. The use of color is also involved in these films at least in a figurative way, and these parallel uses of color can be drawn out with a comparison to *Chromophobia*.

3: *Chromophobia* can also be used alone to illustrate the theme of either communication or freedom in a religious service very effectively. A program that would include slides or tape recorded sound effects to complement or offer a contrast to the theme of the film would also be an imaginative use of the film.

NO TEARS FOR KELSEY

No Tears for Kelsey is a TV style drama that deals directly and forcefully with the communication gap between a young woman and her parents. The film is tightly written and excellently acted. Above all it does not attempt to oversimplify the problem it examines and present us with pat answers.

The major portion of the film is the scene at the Juvenile Hall where Kelsey and her father confront each other and attempt to lay their cards on the table. This high point of

the film is remarkable both for its dramatic control and the highly skilled performances of the actors playing the two roles. The dialog here is also a highpoint of the film. It brings out the unique personalities of the characters while at the same time presenting the universal aspects of their problems.

The conclusion of the film also shows a great deal of imagination. What in effect the film says is that we must try to work out the problem presented in the film for ourselves. There is really no simple formula that will solve all the problems caused by our human failings.

No Tears for Kelsey presents one aspect of the problem of communication very well. It would fit very well in a film program that included *Oh Woodstock* and *Confrontation*. All three films treat the problem of the breakdown in communication between age groups.

28 minutes
Rental—$17.95 color (#1)
   11.95 B&W (#1)
Purchase—$270.00 color (#14)
    135.00 B&W (#14)

Suggestions for the Use of
NO TEARS FOR KELSEY

1: Have four members of the audience play the four major parts that are in the film. This need not be an elaborate production. A simple round table discussion with each part in the film being represented by a member of the audience. The idea is to continue the encounter that is dramatized in the film. The important thing is to keep in character. Develop the character from the evidence we find in the film.

MONEY: THE GREEN FETISH

Money is a drug. Amerika is a drug culture, a nation of crazy addicts. Money can be used for cigarette paper. Roll a joint. Smoke it.

"What do you do?"

That means: "How do you make your money?" Your work is that thing which produces your money. It defines who you are. Our very consciousness is warped by the green fetish!

Money causes the separation between work and life. People don't do what they dig because they want smelly money. People don't dig what they do because they work for the dollar.

No artist ever did it for the bread. If money motivates you, you're not an artist.

People see each other not as human beings, but as financial transactions. The medium is the message. Money corrupts every human relationship it touches.
Jerry Rubin

WHERE WERE YOU DURING
THE BATTLE OF THE BULGE, KID?

Personal integrity in the face of social pressure is the subject of this well written drama. A young man boycotts his high school classes to express what he feels is a moral position. He is supporting a friend, who had been expelled from school for an unpopular political position. His father not understanding the real nature of his son's stands puts pressure on him to conform to the school's regulations.

The father, the son, and the son's friend discuss the situation, and the deeper implications of the problem begin to emerge. Then, unexpectedly, the father finds himself confronted with a moral crisis similar to that of his son's. He is forced to make a hard choice between his own integrity and social convenience. His reaction to this critical situation brings his level of moral awareness to a new level.

The film is specifically designed for promoting discussion of the moral problems it raises. Written, directed, and acted with a great deal of professional competence, it brings alive pertinence of personal integrity.

28 minutes
Rental—$17.95 color (#1)
   11.95 B&W (#1)
Purchase—$270.00 color (#14)
   135.00 B&W (#14)

Suggestions for the Use of
WHERE WERE YOU DURING
THE BATTLE OF THE BULGE, KID?

1: This film is one of the *Insight* series, which are specifically aimed at stimulating discussions of the moral and social issues they raise. As the title of the film might lead one to suspect, it does deal with the generation gap but really only obliquely. The real force of the dramatization lies in the actual moral crises we see enacted on the screen. This film, and the others in the *Insight* series, carefully avoid presenting a neatly packaged answer to the moral issues they explore. As a result they are first rate discussion stimuli.

2: It would be interesting to screen this film with *If There Were No Blacks* and *I'm a Man*. The question of personal integrity and the pressure of society on each of us to make hypocritical adjustments is a central theme of all three films. The different aspects from which they deal with this question would make for an interesting discussion.

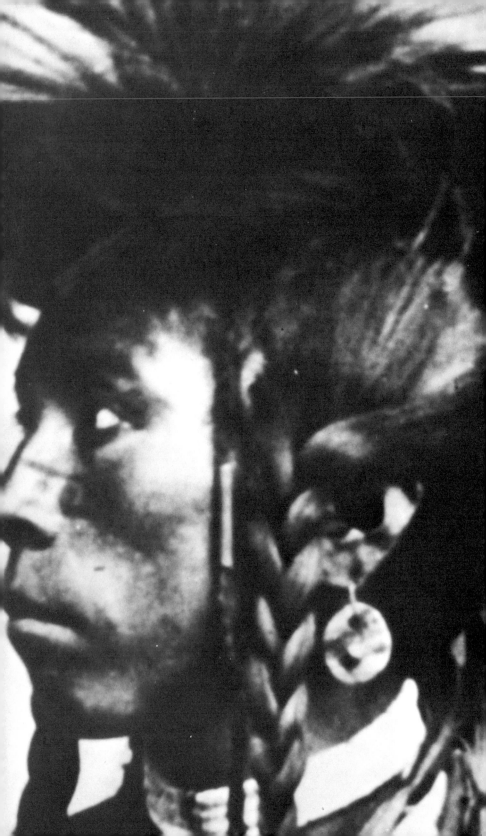

FREEDOM

Freedom's just another word for nothing left to lose.

WHY MAN CREATES

Why Man Creates ranks among the most imaginative and visually fascinating short films to come along in many years. It attempts to explore with a dazzling array of dazzling technical film techniques the experience of what it means to work creatively. The film is in eight sections, each of which would make a short film in itself, and is tied together by the central theme of the varieties of creative experience.

The first section, The Edifice, is a short animated history of ideas. Clever and eye catching, it pictures the development of human intellectual growth as a series of stories on a building. It moves rapidly through the centuries and bombards us with information both on the screen and on the soundtrack.

The second section is a marvelous example of the film maker's visual imagination. It is a pictorial representation of the free flow of ideas with seemingly impossible shots of heads opening up to reveal their contents. The effect is a startling one, and once again the film maker, Saul Bass, uses his technical mastery to get his point across.

The third and fourth sections go together as a pictorial commentary on the task and fate of the artist that explores the seriousness of what the artist does in our world. Is he serious and significant or is he just fooling around?

There is also a section on the struggles and agony of scientific creativity. We share in the experience of a man who has devoted a good part of his life in trying to persuade nature to surrender one of her secrets. This section is a mini drama that is direct and moving.

Why Man Creates is a must for anyone who is interested in getting an audience to appreciate the power and scope of the film medium as a communication device. It is bound to spontaneously create a positive reaction.

25 minutes—color
Rental—$15.00 (#16)
Purchase—$270.00 (#16)

Suggestions for the Use of
WHY MAN CREATES

1: *Why Man Creates* is a highly concentrated package of visual and aural information. Ideally, it should be shown to the same group at least twice with an intervening period of discussion. Each section of the film can be discussed separately both for a simple discovery of all the information that the film maker has given us and also for its implications. The first section, for example, can be analyzed for its point of view. What type of intellectual growth is emphasized? Is the growth of philosophy favorably compared to man's technological advances? What use is made of the soundtrack to get information across and an attitude toward that information?

2: The film because of the variety of its techniques and fullness of its content can be used very well alone as almost a small film festival in itself. It would be a profitable exercise to analyze how each section ties together with those preceding and following it. How the technique in each section is suited to its particular informational content is a subject that should provide hours of profitable discussion.

TURNED ON

Turned On is a short, lyric, visual poem to motion. There is no "meaning" to the film in the sense of social significance, except that beauty contains its own beauty and significance. The film uses shots of sailboats, dune buggies, snowmobiles, and auto racers to create this short poem to the beauty of motion.

The analogy to the poetic form is not a superficial one. The film contains a carefully crafted rhythm and a good deal of visual assonance and alliteration. The editing of the film is the key to the film's substance. What we see on the screen, how long we see it, and in relation to what other shots we have seen and will see is in the final control of the film editor. *Turned On* is an excellent example of the film editor's art.

The film is primarily a mood film. It should be shown in a series of films that would highlight this particular strength of *Turned On*. A strong visual contrast could be created by screening *Turned On* with the NBC documentary, *When Losers Become Winners*. These two films are examples of completely different types of film making both in purpose and style, and would be an excellent introduction into the varieties of the film maker's art.

8 minutes—color
Rental—$10.00 (#16)
Purchase—$120.00 (#16)

Suggestions for the Use of
TURNED ON

1: Have the viewers of the film make a list of adjectives that spontaneously spring to mind during the film. Have as many as possible read them aloud after the screening of the film. How many are similar? How many are radically different?

2: This film, as a mood piece, could be an ideal selection as part of a light show or collage. It would fit well if shown together with a selection of slides shown simultaneously on a separate screen.

STARLIGHT

Because of its experimental nature, *Starlight* is not a universally usable film. Like *Bang Head, Go Bang, Bang* and *One Neetah and Mickey* it should be used with audiences that are relatively sophisticated in their habits of film viewing. Having established its possibility of confusing some audiences, it is a pleasure to recommend the film as one of the most beautiful short films in this book.

The film begins with shots of an old man, an Oriental, walking through a forest. The sound track is a simple chant, which sounds like an Eastern religious song. The atmosphere is pleasantly mysterious. The view we have of the man is from a variety of positions. A series of quick film cuts shows him first from one side then from the rear, as he continues his walk.

Then the scene changes, as the music continues. We are now at what looks like a commune in the country. We now see a series of quick shots of a dog, a child, a mountain, a stream, and the clouds. These shots are repeated, and then the film breaks into color and we view the same scenes in a new way.

The film almost demands that we see it again. It refuses to supply us with the usual literal meaning we have come to expect from a movie. Our way of looking at film is painfully broken down, and we are forced to be receptive to this film in a whole new way.

5 minutes—color-B&W
Rental—$10.00 (#16)
Purchase—$90.00 (#16)

Suggestions for the Use of
STARLIGHT

1: The first thing to do would be to get the general audience reaction to the film. The question here is not so much what the film means, but what the audience feels after viewing it. What is the significance either intellectually or emotionally to the audience of the change in the middle of the film from black and white to color? What does the old man signify? What is the importance of the music in the film? Most of the shots in the film are what is known as tracking shots, i.e., the camera moves along with the subject as it is photographing him. Does this technique add anything to the film? What significance is there, if any, in the old man's smile?

2: *Starlight* can be used with a number of more conventional films such as *The Abandoned, An American Time Capsule* or *Parkinson's Law* to provide a variety of film styles in a program. The atmosphere of the film, as well as its singular style and technique should provide a basis for a profitable discussion.

40

THE FILM DIRECTOR

If, on the other hand, we consider the work of the film director, then it appears that the active raw material is no other than those pieces of celluloid on which, from various viewpoints, the separate movements of the action have been shot. From nothing but these pieces is created those appearances upon the screen that form the filmic representation of the action shot. And thus the material of the film director consists not of real processes happening in real space and real time, but of those pieces of celluloid on which these processes have been recorded. This celluloid is entirely subject to the will of the director who edits it. He can, in the composition of the filmic form of any given appearance, eliminate all points of interval, and thus concentrate the action in time to the highest degree he may require.

Pudovkin, V. I.

CONFRONTATION

On one level this film is about the campus strike that paralyzed San Francisco State College. Taken as such it is an excellent job of film journalism covering, as it does, the multiple factions that went into the makeup of the strike. The film's excellence, though, flows from a deeper level. In *Confrontation* we are presented with a superb analysis of the moral complexities that are part and parcel of our contemporary society.

The San Francisco State crisis is seen in *Confrontation* as a microcosm of America today. The acceleration of every-day living and the awakening of long dormant aspirations in many segments of our society were bound to lead to serious breakdowns in a system that could not or would not adjust. The NBC News Division, the producer of this film, took pains to probe deeply into what happened in this particular instance. In the film we participate in the personal sense of crisis that is felt by a striking professor who feels that he must follow the path he has chosen even though it might end his career. We also spend time sharing the feelings of a dean in the college, who is honestly against the strike, and watch his attempts to manage a difficult situation.

Interspersed throughout the film are excellent shots of the physical confrontations that took place during the whole upheaval. They are expertly used in the film not for sensational effect but for the close contact they constantly give us with the ugly realities of people in conflict.

A radical student, a young girl, is interviewed in depth and we watch her going about the daily events that make up the beginnings of her adult life. A member of the Third World Movement is seen trying to make a breakthrough for his people with some significant action. Establishment politicians also appear to express their views on the situation. Their reactions are

interesting not so much for what they say but for the completely alien value system from which they speak.

Confrontation was originally presented as an hour and a half special on NBC television a few years ago, but it still conveys the same sense of immediacy now as it did then. The agonizing questions of freedom, rights, and justice are presented here in all their contemporary complexity. The film does not present final solutions except to say that the issues involved are a good deal larger than any particular individual or group. No good guys or bad guys emerge; just human beings appear struggling to be honest with themselves and with the society in which they live.

81 minutes—color
Rental—$32.00 (#12)
Purchase—$676.00 (#12)

Suggestions for the Use of
CONFRONTATION

1: The film presents many different points of view about a particular social crisis. It would make for an interesting exercise to assign roles to individual members of the class of the major protagonists in the film. They should try to absorb not just the arguments of the people they are to play but the whole point of view and, if possible, psychological background of that person. After the film a round table discussion could take place with each person playing out his role to the fullest.

2: Divide the audience into separate groups before they see the film. Assign each group to a particular protagonist in the film. Have them write a short impression of the person to whom they are assigned in the film. How does each group's description agree with other descriptions in the same group? What are the differences within each group?

THE VOICES INSIDE

The prison system in the United States is coming in for more and more severe criticism. The whole question of prison is intimately linked with standards in our society that are now being seen as inadequate to a true ideal of justice. *The Voices Inside* is a brief documentary, which gives us an intimate view of the physical and psychological aspects of the reality of putting a man behind bars.

In the film we see the actuality of life in prison and hear the prisoners speak of their situation with a great deal of sensitivity and perception. For all practical purposes we are one of them. Complementing the statements of the prisoners is Dr. Karl Menninger, the noted psychiatrist, who puts the realities expressed by the prisoners in the larger context of the whole moral fabric of American society.

Prison reform, he stresses, is not just misdirected pity but rather the correction of a continuing injustice that affects all of us. To consign a man to prison today is to destroy almost totally a natural resource of our nation. As they stand now, Menninger emphasizes, prisons are our largest producers of hardened criminals, bitter men whom society has perhaps permanently maimed and rendered useless.

22 minutes—color
Rental—$13.00 (#12)
Purchase—$275.00 (#12)

Suggestions for the Use of
THE VOICES INSIDE

1: The problem of prisons and prison reform is the most obvious topic for discussion that the film suggests. It could be screened with *The Insiders,* another film on the same topic by **NBC.**

2: The question of social position and imprisonment is a question that should provide the basis for an interesting discussion. It would be good to include the film as part of a seminar on the subject. The straightforwardness of the film's presentation makes it an excellent information source on the topic it treats.

THE PRICE OF HATING

The price of hating other human beings is loving oneself less. *Indeed, yes. It is a sentence whose spirit rules his book* (Soul on Ice: *Eldridge Cleaver*), *and helps us to gain a sense of the difference between the hatred that shuts men in cages, and the prophetic hatred that responds to keepers and executioners. We have every reason to believe that Cleaver learned to love and accept himself in prison. And through that terrible crystal of his own existence, he came to read the text of the bestial lives of those who created the prisons of the world and then polluted them with their victims. And whose major activity in the world was invariably one or another analogue to this. Cleaver learned, as the book bears witness, that such major activities are a clue to men's major interior activities; the automurder of Western man, the radical inability of this schizoid to put himself together into one man.*

Daniel Berrigan

SCABIES (THE ITCH)

With the simplest of presentations this short animated parable from Yugoslavia makes a rather telling point. We see first a tall, well dressed man in the prime of his life calmly lighting his cigarette while a smooth musical rhythm plays in the background. This scene of contentment is interrupted only when he stops to scratch an annoying itch. His effort results in a little man escaping from his clothing and attempting to run. The large man promptly squashes him.

His composure regained the large man continues his smoking while the music, which had been interrupted, starts again. Then suddenly the man's equanimity is once again interrupted by an annoying itch, this time more seriously. Now he scratches furiously while more and more of the little men try to escape. The violence of his efforts increases as he scratches furiously and tries to crush the growing number of little men who are escaping from his clothing.

Finally, a torrent of little men pour out from under his clothing and flee from his attempts to crush them. Suddenly, the man collapses and nothing is left but a pile of crumpled clothing.

7 minutes—color
Rental—$15.00 (#11)
Purchase—$150.00 (#11)

45

Suggestions for the Use of
SCABIES

1: The moral of the tale isn't too difficult to decipher. Individual freedom is always a bothersome itch. Our contemporary society is full of itches of varying degrees of intensity. The film could well be screened with a film like *Confrontation* or *Reduction* in a seminar that dealt with the problems of individuals and the state. The questions these films treat are extremely current and vitally necessary to an understanding of our society.

2: *Scabies* would be a valuable addition to a series of films that dealt with the technique of the animated film. In *Scabies* the simple though clever use of the soundtrack is a major part of the film's effectiveness.

3: Stop the film before the final exodus of the little people and the collapse of the man. Have the audience write a few lines on what they think the end of the film should be. Discuss these endings after the film is shown completely.

SISYPHUS

The loss of freedom imposed by a creeping materialism is the subject of this short from Yugoslavia. Done with a wry sense of black humor it is a funny and entertaining film. A man sits alone in his room surrounded by his possessions. Slowly but surely they begin to resist his will. A window shade will not stay down, a door will not shut, and a chest of drawers refuses to get itself together.

The point of the film is not just to provide the audience with some slapstick comedy. Rather it is a subtle commentary on the slow encroachment on our freedom that our material goods can exercise. In many more ways than we perhaps care to admit our possessions own us more than we own them. Sisyphus simply draws this truth out to its logical conclusion.

10 minutes—color
Rental—$15.00 (#11)
Purchase—$135.00 (#11)

**Suggestions for the Use of
SISYPHUS**

1: The film could be shown with a great effect with

The Abandoned. **The two films are brief and to the point without being preachy or moralistic. They both deal with an aspect of the power and effect of material goods on man and his society.**

2: The dramatic structure of the film could be discussed. How does the film maker sustain interest in a film that is basically so simple? Is his point too obvious or does he manage to make it real enough to be taken seriously?

BAD DAY

This animated short is strong stuff. It is a fast moving and biting commentary on the absurdity of the human situation. Our deepest freedom is our personal freedom. We are our own worst jailers when we surrender to our own selfishness. *Bad Day* deals with such surrenders with a black humor that borders on the outrageous. It is a short film, just 12 minutes long, but the pace it sets is frenetic, and the film is over before we are able to catch our breaths.

This film should be shown to mature and sophisticated audiences for its best effect. It can't help but get a strong reaction.

12 minutes—color
Rental—$15.00 (#11)
Purchase—$150.00 (#11)

Suggestions for the Use of
BAD DAY

1: This film is most emphatically not a description of the American dream. It is a very sophisticated and sometimes vulgar example of black humor at its best. It is also a very powerful commentary on the ugliness of human selfishness. With the proper audience it is an effective piece of cinema that humorously makes a very serious point. The basically interior nature of real human freedom is a theme that is commented on, at least obliquely, in the film.

2: *Bad Day* provides an excellent bit of comic relief for a situation or discussion that has become too serious. Its 12 minutes of unrelenting slapstick could be the perfect tool to use in turning the mood of a group completely around. As mentioned above it is bound to get a reaction.

$1 + 1 = 3$

What is truth? Is it an independent ideal, or is it something we seek to create to conform to our own selfish interests? In this animated short from Yugoslavia this problem of the nature of truth is wryly dealt with.

A midget sees a sign reading $1 + = 3$. He immediately sets it right to read $1 + = 2$. A giant then happens onto the scene and forces the midget to change the sign back to its original form. Now the midget marshalls all the forces of truth at his command to make the giant see his point. A demonstration with apples in basic arithmatic only arouses the giant's appetite, and he devours one. Great minds of the past are then evoked to help the giant perceive the truth, which only causes him to erupt in a destructive rage.

Finally, the midget is forced to rely on his cleverness as he tries to outwit the giant for the sake of truth. The midget fights a losing battle, however, and the giant's muscle eventually wins out. The final battle for truth, though, has just begun, as a larger giant arrives on the scene.

49

10 minutes—color
Rental—$15.00 (#11)
Purchase—$150.00 (#11)

Suggestions for the Use of
1 + 1 = 3

1: The theme of the film is "might makes right."
The best use of the film, then, would be to have it as a silent
commentary on this aspect of our society. It would fit in very
well with other films that deal with the subtleties and varieties
of oppression. It would add variety to a program that included
I'm a Man and *The Insiders*. It would also provide the core of
a good discussion when screened with *Confrontation* and *Reduction*. Does the theme of this film really apply to the others
or not? Should we restrict the meaning of the film to physical
power, or does it have a wider application? What are some of
the varieties of "might" than can make "right?"

BITTER MELONS

In the middle of this beautiful film about the Gwi tribe, who live in the central Kalahari desert in Botswana, Africa there is a spontaneous native dance that sums up the quiet excellence of this anthropological film. *Bitter Melons* chooses as its focal point the music of the Gwikhwe musician, Ukxone. From his point of view and through his musical artistry we share the daily struggle of the Gwi's to keep alive as the tribe forages for food and water in their unhospitable land.

The beauty of the film is its simplicity. John Marshall, the film maker, does not strive for sensational effects. He simply enters into the lives of Ukxone and his people. *Bitter Melons* is a minor masterpiece of film art.

28½ minutes—color
Rental—$10.00 (#5)

Suggestions for the Use of
BITTER MELONS

1: *Bitter Melons* **is not just another film about natives in their jungle habitat. It is an extremely well made film that deserves to be shown for no other reason than its high level of artistry. It is an anthropological film, a term that has come to be used for those films which are valuable illustrations of the various**

ways in which man lives. The film could be shown with other such films of a similar nature. *Factory, Oh Woodstock,* and *The Sun's Gonna Shine* are other examples of the anthropological film that would fit in very well with *Bitter Melons.*

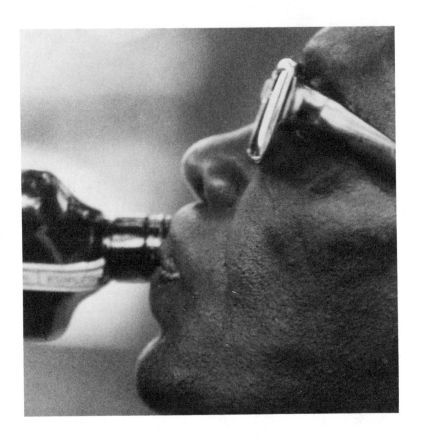

THE BLUES ACCORDIN' TO LIGHTNIN' HOPKINS

Lightnin' Hopkins is a black blues guitar player from the red clay farm country in West Texas. Life for Lightnin' and his friends is simple and basic and the unity of that life with Lightnin's blues is the core of this film.

The beauty of this film is that it simply allows Lightnin' and his friends to be. Lightnin' is old and blind, but the power he radiates as he sips his whiskey, chews his cigar and makes his guitar jump pervades the whole film. Lightnin' plays and he talks and as he does the film brings us the hard life on the red clay that is the reality of which he sings. *Blues* brings us the bittersweet blend of the joy and the pain of life on the land. The country is as poor as the people, and Lightnin' and his friends just manage to scrape a living from the land. But there is beauty here too and a natural joy in life.

We see the black church weatherbeaten and beautiful alone in a field almost like Lightnin' himself. We see also the simple joy he captures with his music as two young black school-girls move smartly down the street. Then we are in a black rodeo with the jump and color that Lightnin' captures on his guitar. Finally, we are at the Saturday night bar-b-que where Lightnin' has played for years, his music the very soul of the life that is there.

Les Blank is the creator of *The Blues Accordin' to Lightnin' Hopkins*. Blank has that rare talent among film makers of not being noticed in his films. Capturing the essence of Lightnin' Hopkins and his music is more than hanging around with a camera and a tape recorder. What to film and how to present it so that the inner reality of the situation is revealed is really shown is at the heart of the art. Les Blank's skill and sensitivity as a film maker are shown to full advantage here and in the other films he has recently made. *The Blues Accordin' to Lightnin' Hopkins* should be seen more than once. The beauty of the character of Lightnin' is worth a careful viewing. Les Blank's skill at letting that beauty speak through the film is worth another.

31 minutes—color
Rental—$50.00 (#9)
Purchase—$400.00 (#9)

Suggestions for the Use of
THE BLUES ACCORDIN' TO
LIGHTNIN' HOPKINS

1: This film is so well made that an analysis of its composition would be most profitable. Preview the film and divide it into sequences, i.e., sections of the film that hold together as a unit either by subject matter emphasized or locations that are shown in the film. Have the audience make a short list of the sequence of shots in each separate sequence. Taking the film a sequence at a time list the new information that each sequence tells us about Lightnin' and his people. It might be good to show each sequence more than once. Then read the lists of information that have been written by the audience members and have them explain how they got the information. Was it stated on the soundtrack literally or figuratively?

Was it just in the visuals shown? Was it a combination of both soundtrack and picture track? After the discussion, which should not be extended for too long a time, show the sequence again.

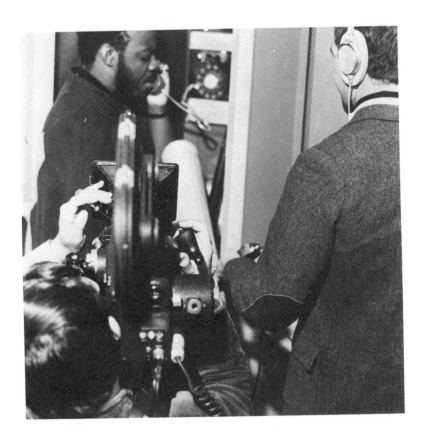

I'M A MAN

This is an angry film. It is a brief but powerful document on what it means to one man to be black. John Barber is a black militant leader, a former president of the New Haven Chapter of the NAACP, a former co-worker with Dr. Martin Luther King, until he split with him over the issue of non-violence, and the founder of the Black Caucus in Hartford Connecticut. He is also far out.

The power and honesty of John Barber are really at the core of this film. In the beginning of the film there is a tragi-comic sequence concerning the stir Barber causes when he insists on walking through town with a dashiki and a spear. At first the flustered reactions of the police and the bewildered expressions on the faces of the townspeople are funny. Then we begin to realize, as the film develops, that Barber's strutting about with a spear really had a serious point. What Barber feels that he and his fellow blacks are suffering from was demonstrated by his walk through the park with a spear. It is a total cultural gap that has survived in this country only by the almost complete suppression of the minority culture. Our current racial problems are not caused by money alone. They go deeper into the question of the freedom of a man to be.

I'm a Man is not just a harangue by a justifiably angry man. It is a sensitive description of a crisis of freedom in our culture that is personified in the man who is John Barber.

20 minutes—color & B&W
Rental—$24.00 (#6)
Purchase—$275.00 (#6)

Suggestions for the Use of
I'M A MAN

1: The film is a penetrating study of what it means to be a black man in a racist society. The concept of racism does not necessarily mean overt prejudice only but can also be expressed in assumed values that form the total social picture. *I'm a Man* gets at these subtler elements of racism in our society in a dramatic yet highly intelligent way. The points the film raises almost automatically lead to a discussion of their implications. What is Barber's point in the film? Is it a valid one or does he overstate his case? Is money the only answer to the race problem? Is total integration of the races?

THE NATIVE

For the black militant in America, it is a simple matter to substitute the word "establishment," which Fanon used in the Algerian context, for "settler," and the word "black" for "native." Thus, when Fanon writes, "The settler pits brute force against weight of numbers . . . His preoccupation with security makes him remind the native out loud that there he alone is master," the American militant nods in knowing agreement and thinks about law and order in the United States.

Not only is the native delimited physically with the help of the army and the police, but, says Fanon, he is also painted as evil. The settler depicts the native society as one

without values, the native as a person insensitive to ethics,
"corrosive, destroying, and disfiguring," indeed "the absolute
evil." While Western values are affirmed, the native is disdained
in bestiary terms: "the stink of the native quarter," his "reptilian
motions," "the breeding swarms."
Horace Sutton

FACTORY

Arthur Barron is a film journalist, who has developed an almost deliberately impersonal style in his films. He attempts to record what he considers to be objective fact and then let that fact speak for itself. The result of this technique is that his films usually have a distinct harshness about them, which strangely enough in no way lessens their fascination for an audience.

Factory is a typical example of his work. It is a filmed report on what goes on in a modestly sized plant in New York City. The plant manufactures rings and employs a number of workers to tend to its machines. The work we see going on is not cruel or even physically trying. It is just that it is dull and stultifying. The men we see are in the humiliating position of serving the machines, which they realize are more valuable than they are. When a machine breaks down, it is an effort to remove and replace it. A man can be removed with the token tribute of a gold ring at a three minute ceremony amid a few nervous laughs.

Arthur Barron's thesis in the film is that the men we see are trapped. They work in an atmosphere where even the quality of their voices becomes inhuman, as it bounces off metal and concrete. They are paid just enough to keep them going, but they are really going nowhere, and the cruel thing is that most of them know it.

56 minutes—B&W
Rental—$40.00 (#8)
Purchase—$225.00 (#8)

Suggestions for the Use of
FACTORY

1: Despite its objective style, *Factory* has a definite point of view. What is the point of view of the film? What are the sights and sounds the film maker uses in his film to get that point of view across to his audience? Is the film fair to the subjects it presents to us on the screen? How can you establish a criterion for fairness in judging such a film?

2: *Factory* is an excellent example of anthropological film making. It details one of the processes of a particular culture. In this case it is a document about the lives of workers in our modern industrial society. As such the film could be shown with great profit together with other anthropological films. *Bitter Melons, Sales Training: Japanese Style, Dead Birds* and *Spend It All* are some of the films that would go into making up an outstanding series of films.

3: Have the audience make a list of adjectives that spring to mind during the film. Read them aloud after the screening of the film and discuss how each list maker arrived at his choices.

FREEDOM AND THE INDIVIDUAL

Freedom has reached a critical point, where, driven by the logic of its own dynamism, it threatens to change into its opposite. The future of democracy depends on the realization of the individualism that has been the ideological aim of modern thought since the Renaissance. The cultural and political crisis of our day is not due to the fact that there is too much individualism but that what we believe to be individualism has become an empty shell. The victory of freedom is possible only if democracy develops into a society in which the individual, his growth and happiness, is the aim and purpose of culture, in which life does not need any justification in success or anything else, and in which the individual is not subordinated to or manipulated by any power outside of himself, be it the State or the economic machine; finally, a society in which his conscience and ideals are not the internalization of external demands, but are really his and express the aims that result from the peculiarity of his self.
Erich Fromm

PARKINSON'S LAW

The creeping monster of bureaucracy, a self justifying, all embracing reality in our contemporary society, is the satirical subject of this Yugoslavian short. The premise of the film is simple and to the point. A man works diligently at a small lathe. His work is the one practicality in the film. Eventually he is joined by an administrator and administrative assistants. This administrator then leads to the presence of a supervisor, who brings with him statisticians, stenographers, bookkeepers, clerks and other assorted faceless cogs in the bureaucratic machine. Slowly but surely, the reason for the existence of this complicated framework, the lathe operator, is forced off the screen. The organization, self sustaining and omnipresent, takes up the whole picture having been completely cut off from the real reason for their existence.

The question of the difficulty of real freedom in such a society, bound up as it is in such complexity of detail, is one

possible aspect of the film that could make *Parkinson's Law* a stimulating basis for discussion.

12 minutes—B&W
Rental—$12.50 (#11)
Purchase—$125.00 (#11)

Suggestions for the Use of
PARKINSON'S LAW

1: Ideally, the film should be shown as part of a series. The film gets its point across very effectively, but would be too simple in itself to produce much discussion mileage. It would be an excellent film to show with *The Selling of the Pentagon* **which touches on the same theme of bureaucratic complexity.**

2: The film is also interesting for its technique. It is not an animated film, but the use of multiple images and other special effects make it a unique visual experience. This basic effect of the film could be reproduced by photographing rearranged still shots for a few seconds apiece with a super 8 motion picture camera.

DREAMS AND SCHEMES

Six sight gags each dealing with the theme of human frustration make up this collection of animated shorts that are prime examples of the sweet and sour taste of black humor. The film provides an ideal counterpoint to longer, more socially serious films and makes for an excellent change of pace.

One example would give an idea of the general tenor of the films. A prisoner is shown painstakingly burrowing out of his cell to an open field beyond the prison walls. Freed at last from the gray monotony of his confinement, he discovers to his horror that the prospect of freedom is too much for him to absorb. Terrified he quickly scurries back to the more comfortable security of his prison cell.

Dreams and Schemes is not meant to be analyzed for its philosophical profundity. This mini festival of black humor is simply meant to be enjoyed for itself.

6 minutes—color
Rental—$15.00 (#11)
Purchase—$150.00 (#11)

1: The film provides a good deal of humor that could be a welcome relief from a discussion that has become weighted down with its own seriousness. If used properly, *Dreams and Schemes* could restore the correct psychological balance to a series of films dealing with social problems. Really the film's ultimate comment is that there is a great deal of raw comedy in the human situation.

2: *Dreams and Schemes,* despite its ironic and semi-serious look at human nature, was composed with a good deal of craftsmanship and talent. It is an excellent film to use in discussing the structure and workings of the sight gag. It would also fit in well with a series of films that stressed the techniques and uses of the animated film. What happens on the soundtrack during each of the films? How does this sound information, we receive, influence the effect of the film? Are there any pictures or sounds in the film that are extraneous, i.e., really could be removed without lessening the impact of the film?

THE BALLAD OF THE CROWFOOT

This film is a poetic lament on the passing of a way of life. The film's producers, The National Film Board of Canada, selected and trained a group of Crowfoot Indians to make this film from their point of view. It was directed by Willie Dunn, a Crowfoot, who also wrote the ballad which is the core of the film.

The film opens with a skillful collection of still photographs, which have been made into a moving montage of images. Through them we see the lives of a people that were. Then we see live motion picture footage of the lives of the Crowfoot. The long history of alien encroachment and constant betrayal is recalled by the descendants of its original victims. Throughout the film, the sad lament of the plight of his people is sung by Willie Dunn. "Crowfoot, Crowfoot, why the tears? / You've been a brave man for many years. / Why the sadness? / Why the sorrow? / Maybe there'll be a better tomorrow."

The film is a powerful presentation of a problem that refuses to go away. It is a well made document that gets the audience into the experience of what it means to be an alien in one's own land.

61

10 minutes—B&W
Rental—$10.00 (#6)
Purchase—$80.00 (#6)

Suggestions for the Use of
THE BALLAD OF THE CROWFOOT

1: This film would most obviously be of use in a series of films on racial injustice in general or the injustices done to the Indians in particular. As such it would go very well with *Between Two Rivers* and *Ishi in Two Worlds* in dealing with the Indian problem. It's deeper psychological aspects, i.e., what it means to be part of an alien culture surrounded by foreigners to one's habits and customs, could be supplemented by screening the film along with *I'm a Man.*

2: What are the full dimensions of oppression? Is it simply a physical phenomenon, or does it have more subtle connotations? What are these connotations from the evidence we see presented in the film?

3: What about the effectiveness of the film's technique? Does it help or hinder what the film is trying to say? Is the soundtrack, the ballad, helpful to the purpose of the film?

4: Have the audience write a short list of qualities or characteristics describing the stereotype of the Indian. Do this first list before the film is screened. Write another after the film is shown. Compare the two.

A NOTE FROM ABOVE

At first viewing this animated short might be taken as a thoroughly irreligious film. Actually, the point of the film is much more subtle and, unfortunately, historically valid.

A cloud hovers in the heavens from which drop little notes to earth. The people, who rush to gather them up, take them as divine directives and fall over each other in their rush to carry them out. Finally, there is one that reads: "Thou shalt kill." Without the slightest hesitation the people below carry it out, annihilating each other in the process. After the slaughter is over, and a graveyard silence comes over the scene, one last note flutters to the ground. It reads: "Thou shalt *not* kill. Sorry—my mistake!"

2 minutes—color
Rental—$10.00 (#11)
Purchase—$100.00 (#11)

1: The concept of having God on one's side is as old as man. What does the film have to say about this notion? Can the love of God and the love of man ever conflict? Why is such stress put on the idea that communism is godless? Is this emphasis on godlessness a product of theological examination, or does it spring from other motivations? What is the point of the film? Is it irreligious? Why are religious hatreds such a violent social force? Are they really religious at all?

THE INSIDERS

Despite some of its technical imperfections, this film about prison life draws its power from the fact that it was made by the inmates of a prison themselves. The story it tells is not a pleasant one, as we see a first hand visual record of the slow grinding down of men to the level of brutes.

The soundtrack is a narration by one of the prisoners. It details the daily experience of life behind bars. Scene after scene we see and hear the examples of animal cunning that the inmates are forced to use to survive in this atmosphere. Everyone has his own hustle, his shrewd control over his fellow prisoners that he employs with animal cunning just to get by from day to day. The simplest necessities of life become things to be schemed for, and the psychological tension of the atmosphere becomes more real than the prison bars.

The film is a view of prison life that is simple in its presentation, but devastating in its dramatic impact.

26 minutes—color
Rental—$13.00 (#12)
Purchase—$275.00 (#12)

Suggestions for the Use of
THE INSIDERS

1: Any discussion of the problems of prison reform would be greatly enhanced by the screening of *The Insiders*. Its sense of immediacy more than makes up for any failure of technical sophistication. It could also be shown with *The Voices Inside*, another film on the same subject, with great effect.

2: The concept of psychological freedom is important here. The men are physically restricted by their confinement, but their freedom is more seriously restricted than this. Point out some of these deeper manifestations of the prisoners' loss of freedom. These questions could also be discussed in greater depth, if *The Insiders* were to be shown with *Factory* and *I'm a Man*. How the theme of the necessity of true human freedom for survival as men is common to all three films would be an excellent viewpoint from which to discuss them.

The Greatest Article I Read in My Whole Life

Richard Nixon's Vice President, Spiro Agnew, writing about Attica under his byline in The New York Times newspaper the other day, said: "To compare the loss of life by those who violate society's law with the loss of life of those whose job it is to uphold it—represents not simply an assault on human sensibility but an insult to reason."

Beautiful. I think it was the greatest article I read in my whole life. Governor Rockefeller seems to feel the way Agnew does, but Rockefeller has a family background for things like this. The Ludlow massacre and all that. Agnew's terrific article came from the heart. Because of it I finally was able to brush off the last shreds of the stupid ideas Sister Anna Gertrude outfitted us with in St. Benedict Joseph Labre School, Queens, New York City.

That silly Jesus Christ. The way that old nun made us learn it, Jesus spent the whole last morning of His life standing in Part XXXII with a real bum named Barabbas. Instead of making a deal to sink Barabbas, Christ stood around rooting for Barabbas to get his case severed and dropped. One description of Barabbas was that he was a boss of thieves in Jerusalem. The first Jewish button man. I used to sit in class and picture Barabbas as Lepke with a big beard.

Another thing I read said Barabbas actually was indicted for being the leader of a revolutionary movement, the Zealot Movement, which wanted to overthrow Rome. One of these demonstrations got rough and a guy died and the law grabbed Barabbas. Whichever version is right, Barabbas was under a heavy indictment and he was given amnesty and we were taught that it was a great thing, the way Christ was happy to see Barabbas get off. But now, reading Agnew, I can see what Christ really was. He should have figured, here, this guy next to me is only a number and nobody is going to get excited if he goes. Then Christ should have maneuvered the judge and crowd so they would let him go and make a party cutting Barabbas's head off.

Let's go to the afternoon. Here He is hanging on a cross all afternoon and what does He do? He spends most of his time talking to two thieves they have hanging alongside Him. Sister Anna Gertrude used to get tears in her eyes reading from Luke. And, look at the way this Christ, in a life-and-death situation, worried about thieves. Finally, one of the thieves, I put him down in my mind as a top hoodlum like Bumpy Johnson, said: "Lord, remember me when you come into your Kingdom."

And Jesus Christ, in what I was taught was the last line He said on earth, turned to this thief, this Bumpy Johnson, and said: "This day you will be with me in paradise."

How do you like it? How do you like what some backward nun put into my head? Here's a Guy has nails in Him and He is wasting His time giving amnesty to a thief, and they had me believing for a long time, Sister Anna Gertrude and the other nuns in St. Benedict Joseph Labre School, Queens, New York City, that this Jesus Christ was great because He died thinking of thieves. I should have spent my time looking at dirty pictures.

At least now, because of Spiro Agnew's terrific article, I know that thieves should be regarded in a crisis as ciphers to be killed and barely counted and never mourned. There are three real good prayer people who get their pictures taken with Richard Nixon and Spiro Agnew and it would be marvelous to hear them say something about Agnew's terrific article, just in case there are

many people whose thinking has been crippled by faulty religious upbringing. It would help straighten this whole Attica question out if the three really good prayer people, Billy Graham, Norman Vincent Peale and Terence Cooke, would comment on Agnew's article, and how silly Jesus Christ was.
Jimmy Breslin

THE PRISONER
"... the parole board injustices are visited upon a group of people that have no representation. It is the problem with the prison system in general. Usually someone who goes to jail does not know anybody who "counts." We are now beginning to see more concern about the prison system because, with the marijuana violations, the middle class is being introduced to the prison structure. But still, preponderantly, the prisoner is an impotent man with no access to the Establishment, the media, or the government."
Willard Gaylin

PEACE

Though the glory of war may be great and ancient glory it is not the final glory of God.
George Bernard Shaw

This is an oddly unsettling film. It's power lies almost entirely in its straight reporting of the major political events of the 1960's. Its effect as a film, however, is much more than a simple informational exercise. What strikes the viewer almost immediately is the tremendously tumultuous nature of the years we have somehow just lived through.

Sander Vanocour brings us back to the beginnings of it all with the Nixon-Kennedy debates of 1960. Then we are led through the tragedy of Dallas and the unforgettable funeral once again. Barry Goldwater is resurrected as we see the scenario of the 1964 elections reenacted against the background of the growing disaster in Vietnam and the ever increasing restlessness of the Civil Rights Movement at home.

Finally, we move to the turmoil of 1968, Bobby Kennedy, Eugene McCarthy, and Senator Abe Ribicoff's speech at the Chicago Convention.

What the film captures well is the almost chaotic condition of our contemporary society. It is an ideal tool not just for use as a quick historical review of recent events but as a portrait of a society where peace is a precious commodity. The United States is a powerful country, and one of the reasons it is powerful is the raw, naked energy that is present within its borders. That energy in all its power and its ever present threat of danger is captured in *When Losers Become Winners*.

14 minutes—B&W
Rental—$7.00 (#12)
Purchase—$135.00 (#12)

Suggestions for the Use of
WHEN LOSERS BECOME WINNERS

1: This film could provide the raw material for an analysis of how a short summary type film is put together. Analyze the shots the film maker uses and try to come up with reasons why they were chosen and why they were used in the order you see on the screen.

2: We usually think of violence as physical violence, someone getting roughed up or killed. What other types of violence are presented in the film?

3: How would you relate this film to a theme of peace?

Is the film a peaceful one? How can a person find peace in a society as hectic as the one the film presents?

4: The quotation from *The Selling of the President 1968* can really be applied to each of the major figures appearing in the film. What do techniques such as cited by McGinniss tell us about our society? Is being careful to please everybody a way to achieve peace, or does the building of peace sometimes strangely involve a violent struggle?

THE SELLING OF THE PRESIDENT

Ailes had been sent to Chicago three days before Nixon opened the fall campaign. His instructions were to select a panel of questioners and design a set. But now, on the day of the program, only six hours, in fact, before it was to begin, Ailes was having problems.

His biggest problem was with the panel. Shakespeare, Treleaven and Garment had felt it essential to have a "balanced" group. First, this meant a Negro. One Negro. Not two. Two would be offensive to whites, perhaps to Negroes as well. Two would be trying too hard. One was necessary and safe. Fourteen percent of the population applied to a six- or seven-member panel, equaled one . . . Texas would be tricky, though. Do you have a Negro and a Mexican-American, or if not, then which?
Joe McGinniss

SUNDAY PICNIC

This film is perhaps the most difficult in this book to fathom. It is not recommended, then, for use with a class not well versed in symbolic film. *Sunday Picnic* is an allegory, and as such demands an interpretation to be understood and appreciated. We see a group of people in a country field idling away, from what we may understand from the title of the film, a Sunday afternoon. Dressed in clothes that were stylish around the turn of the century, they are a study in idle complacency.

A dignified matron sits in a wicker chair, a man in late middle age naps in a bed, which is protected from the sun by a tent, while another man is taking careful aim with his rifle at a target of paper pinned to a tree. We also see a young girl swimming in a nearby pond while a quartet of musicians plays the same slow waltz over and over again in the middle of the field.

71

The scene goes on uninterrupted for about five minutes until finally a newcomer comes on the scene. A young man, the girl's lover, has arrived to keep a rendezvous with her. The musicians momentarily stop their music, then caught up in the new lively mood of the scene, begin to play a livelier piece. This change in the musical mood awakens the sleeping man, who at the urging of the older woman gets the musicians to resume their boring waltz music. Just as they begin to obey him a shot

rings out, and the target shooter holds up his target with a bull's eye.

Then inexplicably the elderly man tries to remove the target shooter's gun but is prevented by the girl's lover. After this interruption the scene reverts to what it had been at the beginning. Only one thing changes; the older woman walks off the field. The boring waltz music begins once more.

13 minutes—B&W
Rental—$15.00 (#11)
Purchase—$150.00 (#11)

1: This is definitely not a film that lends itself to an easy interpretation or facile use in the classroom to get some point across. When used with a class that is used to analyzing films, it can be most interesting and effective. Have the group view the film and then write down in a few lines their general impression of the total effect of the film. Then have them all read aloud to see if there is some consensus as to how the film affected them. Then show the film again and try to analyze the important parts of the film, for example, the significance of the main characters, to see if a pattern of meaning can be worked out in the film.

2: View the film without the soundtrack. Then show the film again with the track. Try to discern what the soundtrack adds to the meaning of the film.

TUMULT, TURMOIL, AND TURBULENCE

No account of the 1960's would be complete without taking serious note of the great acceleration in the rise and development of the Civil Rights Movement. This country came to realize that there was much more at stake here than the simple matter of seating arrangements on a public bus. The question of even simple equality before the law was discovered to be a total question for each of us personally, the implications of which are still with us today.

Tumult, Turmoil, and Turbulence is a capsulized history of the philosophical growth and development of the Civil Rights Movement in the United States from the early sit-ins in Birmingham through the Poor Peoples' March on Washington to the confrontations at Cornell University. Frank McGee narrates the film and attempts to give us a sense of direction in the sequence of events that the film presents on the screen. Martin Luther King appears as does Stokely Carmichael. The Black Panthers and their problems with the police are brought up, and an attempt is made to put them into context.

The film does not pretend to answer the problems it illustrates with slick oversimplifications. Rather it is an invaluable tool for providing the raw information of the struggle for black equality in an intelligible context.

13 minutes—B&W
Rental—$7.00 (#12)
Purchase—$135.00 (#12)

Suggestions for the Use of
TUMULT, TURMOIL, AND TURBULENCE

1: This is an ideal film for the discussion of the whole question of the Civil Rights Movement in the United States. Ideally it could be used with *I'm a Man* and *If There Were No Blacks* for a small film seminar on the subject of the problems of race in the United States.

2: Since the film takes the form of a capsulized summary of the Civil Rights Movement, it provides a good basis for an historical review of the subject. What men and what methods have provided the most effective way for achieving racial justice in this country? Has there been any real progress in this area or are the problems we face today the same as we faced twenty years ago? Does the film present a fair overview of the subject or does it oversimplify matters?

UNLIMITED OPPORTUNITIES
Unlimited opportunities can be as potent a cause of frustration as a paucity or lack of opportunities. When opportunities are apparently unlimited, there is an inevitable depreciation of the present . . . Patriotism, racial solidarity, and even the preaching of revolution find a more ready response among people who see limitless opportunities spread out before them than among those who move within the fixed limits of a familiar, orderly and predictable pattern of existence.
Eric Hoffer

THE DAY JACK PITTMAN DIED

This is a film about a small town's reaction to the death of another one of its young citizens in Vietnam. The small town in question is Beallsville, a small farming town in southern Ohio. It was selected as a subject for the film because when the film was made Jack Pittman was the fifth young man to die from Beallsville, a fact which made the death rate of men from

Beallsville in Vietnam 76 times the national average.

The Day Jack Pittman Died tells the story of small town, USA. The questions that are disturbing America, everything from long hair to the threat of world Communism all come to the surface in Beallsville. The film poignantly shows the town's reactions to the death of the young men, especially Jack Pittman's. There is real suffering here not just from the deaths of its young

men, but also from the agonizing reexamination of its values that the town goes through.

The film communicates on many levels. First, there are the people we see in the film trying to be honest and sincere in what they believe, yet caught in their own inner conflicts and trying to resolve them in a world turned upside down. Then there is the subtle camerawork which visually juxtaposes the conflicts of values that the citizens of Beallsville are struggling with. It is not difficult to see that we too live in Beallsville.

26 minutes—color
Rental—$15.00 (#12)
Purchase—$330.00 (#12)

Suggestions for the Use of
THE DAY JACK PITTMAN DIED

1: This film has a definite point of view or attitude towards its subject matter. How does the selection of shots in the film help to make that point?

2: What is the basic conflict in the film? Does that conflict apply only to Beallsville or is it more widespread?

3: Is the film one sided or does it try to be completely balanced in reporting on what it finds in Beallsville? What are the reasons for your attitude towards the film? Can you point to specific shots or sequences of shots that provide the film with its point of view?

MOODS OF SURFING

As the title suggests, this is a mood film, a poem rather than a thesis. Its message, if one can speak of a message, is definitely non-verbal. It speaks rather to our sense of rhythm and color, and the skill of the film maker lets us see in a sense what peace is.

It would be most instructive to show this film along with a more explicit film such as *When Losers Become Winners* or *The Day Jack Pittman Died*. These latter two films are more verbal in what they have to say. They both have an explicit point to make. *Moods of Surfing* communicates in a different way but in a manner that is no less real. How the film communicates itself to the viewer, the techniques it uses and does not use, would make the use of the film an enriching experience.

15 minutes—color
Rental—$12.00 (#16)
Purchase—$150.00 (#16)

Suggestions for the Use of
MOODS OF SURFING

1: The questions of how and what a film communicates are important here. There is no thesis or message really in *Moods of Surfing.* **It is more like a lyric poem that tries to capture an aspect of simple beauty rather than present a point. It is important to remember this when approaching** *Moods of Surfing* **and films similar to it.**

2: The film can be used as a mood piece, something like a simple pictorial background for a multi-media show. The central part of the show whether it be slides or a singer could occupy center stage, while this film is played on a side screen.

3: The way the film creates its mood can be analyzed by paying attention to what individual shots the film maker uses, how long he keeps them on the screen, and finally, in what order he decides to show them. By studying these elements in the film a deeper appreciation of the film maker's art can be achieved.

THE MAGICIAN

The Magician is a powerful allegory on the horror of war. The point of this film is not so much the fact that war is physically destructive but that it entails a psychological corruption that far outweighs its physical effects. In this case the psychological corruption involves children who are led slowly and patiently from innocence to psychological and physical death.

The film begins with a group of children playing on what appears to be a deserted beach. They come upon an amuse-

ment stand which is run by an older man who charms them with his wizardry. At first he entices them with a collection of magic tricks. Then he gradually gets them involved with marching to the exciting tempos of military music and then shooting at targets in his shooting gallery. He is the picture of patience and concern as he slowly gets them to do his will. The moving targets become little dolls as the children continue to shoot. Soon they are totally caught up in their new activity, and they give little resistance to his promptings as he leads them over a nearby hill to participate in the real thing. He then returns alone to begin the cycle all over again.

The strength of the film lies in its meticulously planned power of suggestion. The evil of the film takes place in an atmosphere of deceptive innocence. The horrors that go on are interior horrors and the minds of the children are slowly but surely transformed by the subtly charming magician. The film also allows us to complete its meaning, as it were, with our own imaginations. We don't see a single war scene directly. They all take place on the other side of the hill. All we see is the power of the magician's personality as he works his will upon the children's innocence. We are able to make all the necessary parallels to our own worlds in our own minds. As we make these parallels, we see how valid the point of the film is. There is a secret delight in all of us in the game of war with its stirring music and promise of excitement. We like the children are easily led by the magician whatever appearance he may choose to assume.

The Magician is a powerfully direct film, which totally engages us from its very first moment to its rigorously logical conclusion.

13 minutes—B&W
Rental—$12.50 (#11)

Suggestions for the Use of
THE MAGICIAN

1: What is an allegory and in what sense can *The Magician* be said to be an allegory?

2: *The Magician* is a strong anti-war film that is essentially symbolic in its style and presentation. It might be interesting to show this film in conjunction with a more literal one such as *The Day Jack Pittman Died* and compare how two different styles of film get their meaning across.

3: *The Magician* was made by a Polish film maker whose view of war is slightly different from what ours might be expected to be. Is it possible to say something about the necessity of war after our country's experience in Vietnam?

DEAD BIRDS

Dead Birds is a slow sensitive study of the Dani, a Stone Age tribe living in Western New Guinea. Its beauty and effectiveness as a film lies in its painstaking faithfulness to and respect for the lives of the people it is recording. It is a film made with such sensitive understanding that it is fast becoming a classic of its kind.

Living in a land virtually untouched by modern civilization the days of the Dani are taken up with the endless cycle of wresting survival from nature and from the immediately neighboring tribe with whom they wage an endless and bloody war. The central focus of the film is this never ending battle the Dani wage with their neighbors. This warfare from which the possibility of a sudden death from an enemy raid is an everyday reality is almost an allegory for Dani existence. The world they know is an impersonal and dangerous one, and the constant battle they wage with their fellow men is but a symbolic struggle to assert themselves in a savage milieu that can be fickle and capricious with life and death.

The film concentrates on the daily routine of a Dani male warrior. We follow him in the morning to his watchtower post, as he takes up his daily duties guarding against an enemy attack. We then see the Dani women leave for their work in the fields while the Dani children play at being men nearby.

Then we see the battle sequence, a highly formalized ritual where death from an enemy spear is everpresent, but where a highly dramatic show of manhood is even more important. The battle can be, and often is, an all day affair. It courses back and forth on the flat plain of no man's land between the two villages. Highly decorated young warriors make repeated dashes to the enemy lines dodging spears and hurling their own until they are forced back by a similar attack from their adversaries. The battle finally ends when a warrior is killed or wounded. The war, though, goes on endlessly, since it is a point of honor that the fallen warrior must eventually be avenged.

The strongest impression the film makes is the unrelenting savagery of the life of the Dani people. They are locked in an endless cycle of wresting survival from nature and avenging their dead. Subtly, though, other elements arise. The Dani, for all their primitive savagery, are a beautiful people. Their physical nakedness parallels their psychological nakedness in the face of the brutality of life. Their life style, which on the surface seems so different from ours, is in many ways more rational and life respecting than our more advanced forms of living together. The code of life they have adopted does not spring from an arbitrary love of violence but rather from a need to come to grips with a savage environment. It helps them make sense of their world and supports them in their daily lives. Strange and horrible to us at first, the life style of the Dani slowly emerges as in many ways more civilized than many aspects of our contemporary urban existences. *Dead Birds* is a story of man.

83 minutes—color
Rental—$45.00 (#6)
Purchase—$450.00 (#6)

THE MODERN CORPORATION
Every modern corporation has its camp in addition
to its hunting bands. It contains all those who are not actually

devising, making, and selling the product that brings in the money. They may be physically only just across the corridor, but in all other ways they are in a different world. They are in departments with names like finance, personnel, planning, public relations, administration, registry, welfare, and so on; and, however devoted their efforts, however valuable their contribution, the members of the hunting bands look on them as the "women and children" of the corporation. Any hunter who is sweating his guts out to meet a production or copy deadline or a sales target thinks of them as, to some extent, a burden that he and his fellows have to carry, and I suspect that there is even a submerged feeling that it is women's work they are doing. Healthy, strong, active men ought to be sharing the exertions and perils of the hunt, not skulking in the warmth and safety of the camp all day. It is very difficult to say who in the corporation is in the camp. and who is in the hunting band—but only if you are in the camp.
Antony Jay

Suggestions for the Use of
DEAD BIRDS

1: Since it is rather expensive, *Dead Birds* ideally should be shown to a large group to get the maximum benefit from the film rental. *Dead Birds* is what is known as an anthropological film, i.e., it presents us with a detailed study of how man lives in his everyday coping with life. Ideally the film then should be shown as a part of a series of such films. Some others would be *The Voices Inside, Between Two Rivers, The Day Jack Pittman Died,* and *Oh Woodstock.* The different aspects of human behavior in various social systems could then be studied and compared.

2: Violence is a factor of society that is present in all cultures. The violence in *Dead Birds* may appear to be shocking and completely foreign to our modern experience at first, but on reflection may not be all that foreign after all. What are the reasons for the Dani's customs and habits, especially the savage warfare that is a constant factor in their lives? Is this warfare completely irrational, or are there parallels to it in our modern society?

3: The style of the film is interesting. The skill of the film maker allows us to get very close to the people we are seeing on the screen. Does this style add anything to the film that a more distanced approach would give?

81

4: Does the film have a point of view or attitude towards what it is trying to portray? What is this attitude and how is it brought out on the screen?

5: What is our attitude towards the Dani at the end of the film? Is it one of superiority, pity, disgust, admiration? Why?

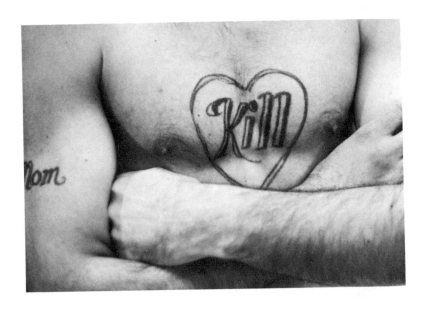

REDUCTION

Reduction is a biting satire on the process of being inducted into the military. Shot in the farm country outside of Chicago in 1967, this stark, surrealistic film has as its theme the experience of a farm boy undergoing his first contact with the military machine. The visual metaphor in the film is the comparison of men being inducted into the army and sheep being led to slaughter. The sheep are sheared, and the men are stripped for their medical. The sheep docilely await slaughter, and the men obediently troop off to war.

There is a haunting quality to the film that invests even the most ordinarily pleasant pastoral shots with a deathly chill. The texture of the film is almost clammy as the boy is pulled further and further into the impersonal world of spit and polish. What we are seeing is a slow death, not with the spattering of blood and guts, but rather with the gradual infusion of embalming fluid into his body.

10 minutes—B&W
Rental—$10.00 (#4, #7, #10)
Purchase—Inquire (#4, #7, #10)

Suggestions for the Use of
REDUCTION

1: This film has a definite point of view. What are the means that the film maker uses to get that point of view across?

2: Is the film just about being inducted into the army or does it have a wider comment on our society? What is this wider commentary? Is it clear from the film?

3: What is the basic metaphor of the film and how is it brought out? Can you design a film that uses another metaphor and would be suited to getting the same point across?

4: How does the film maker cut his film, i.e., how does he select the length and sequence of his film to get his point across?

5: How do the various camera angles affect the film, that is, why does the film maker choose to shoot each shot the way he does, e.g., from above or below the eye level of his subjects, close to the subject, a medium distance or far from the subject?

EFFECTS OF THE WAR

The war indeed has been a long loneliness. It has brought us too much knowledge and little consolation, too much protest, too little joy. We know too much about Vietnam, too much about American moral savagery, too much about hedonists, too much about puritans, too much about polltakers, taxpayers, and warmakers. So much indeed that we must begin again to unwind and unlearn, to waste many hours, if we are to have anything new to offer the times. It is necessary that some, perhaps even wasting time, will become contemplatives, that is to say, men of profound and available sanity.
Daniel Berrigan, S.J.

83

CONCERT FOR HIS MAJESTY

This film is a brief ironic commentary on the
cynicism of power politics. It is the capsulized history of how a
powerful king threatened by an imminent revolution manages to
remain in control of the situation. The king is the personification
of self-serving greed through his oppressive domination of his
subjects. When idealistic revolutionary forces are set in motion
by his policies, he demonstrates the instinctive sense of self-
preservation that is the true mark of a politician. By clever
manipulation of the forces that he senses are operative in his
society he manages not only to survive but to become the leader
of the revolution that seeks to overthrow him.

For all its cleverness *Concert for His Majesty* is not
a fantastic film. The shrewdness of the king in being in the right
place and with the right people at the right time is the characteris-
tic of the true political animal. The force of this animated short
is that it compresses the process of political hypocrisy. We are
not allowed to forget what the king once stood for due to the
passage of time or our own short political memories. *Concert for
His Majesty* would go well in a film program that also included
NBC's *When Losers Become Winners,* which covers similar
territory but in a documentary fashion.

7 minutes—color
Rental—$15.00 (#11)
Purchase—$135.00 (#11)

84

1: This film is an animated short, or for want of a better phrase, an adult cartoon. As such it would be an excellent addition to a short film festival on animation. Such films could include *Why Man Creates*, which includes sections that are animated, *Homo Homini, Bags*, and many of the films of Norman McClaren. No great expertise in the mechanical techniques of animation is an absolute necessity to run such a festival. Rather the common audience reactions to the films presented and a discussion of why animated shorts get the reaction they do would be a fruitful result of such a festival.

2: *Concert for His Majesty*, as an animated short, also would provide a touch of variety to a collection of films dealing with social and political problems. The film is included in this section devoted to peace because it points up a basic problem in the attempts at improving the conditions of any given society. There are always opportunists about, indeed, there is a touch of opportunism in each one of us, that is able to corrupt the noblest of causes. *Concert for His Majesty* is an excellent satiric exposition of that hypocrisy.

BAGS

It is almost always a powerful dramatic device to see base human characteristics stripped of their human camouflage and presented in their basic naked ugliness. Tadeusz Wilkosz, a Polish film maker, has cleverly animated the normal castoff rubbish in an attic and invested it with human characteristics. The junk that one would expect to find simply lying about suddenly becomes alive, each piece with a destructive will of its own.

Wilkosz has made his film a clever allegory on greed. The device he employs of using castoff junk as his main characters heightens the basic effect of outward ugliness reflecting the inner wasteland that supports violence and greed.

Bags is included in the section on Peace because it explores and illustrates the contrary. The selfishness that leads to violence is ugly, perhaps uglier than the final physical manifestation of violence itself. *Bags* is a clever testimony to that reality.

9 minutes—color
Rental—$12.00 (#16)
Purchase—$120.00 (#16)

Suggestions for the Use of
BAGS

1: An allegorical film is usually an excellent basis for discussion because its power of suggestion is so rich. Why did the film maker choose the device of old junk in an attic to animate his film? More importantly perhaps is the question of the effectiveness of this technique. How does it add or subtract from the effect the film maker wants to achieve?

2: If possible *Bags* should be part of a series of films that deal with violence. It would be an excellent contrast to screen *Bags* with *The Anderson Platoon* or with *When Losers Become Winners*. The themes of these three films all deal with violence. The way the film maker presents his subject matter, though is different in each case. *Bags* is an allegorical treatment of violence that illustrates the raw naked ugliness of violence. *The Anderson Platoon*, despite the fact that it follows an infantry platoon through combat, shows the dull, unrelenting boredom of warfare, and *When Losers Become Winners* gives us a capsulized picture of the struggles for political power, which are really violence of a special sort.

AN AMERICAN TIME CAPSULE

This is the film of Charles Braverman which you might well have seen on The Smothers Brothers Show in the fall of 1968. Its strength lies in its unique style coupled with a subject matter that suits its technique perfectly. Basically the film is a rapid succession of still photographs from American history which have been filmed and then cut together. The effect is that the viewer sees American history from its very beginnings to the present flash before him like a chemical reaction.

Psychologically the film pounds us with visual images and associations that at first might leave us bewildered with a sensory overload. Gradually, though, we find ourselves able to step up our perceptions to keep pace with what we are seeing on the screen. Even though the images appear on the screen only for fractions of a second, we not only grasp them but are able to relate them to what we have already seen. The complex interrelationships of our American past with its awesome displays of power become much clearer in the three minutes that *An American Time Capsule* flashes before us on the screen.

The film is eminently usable for many purposes. It is, first of all, an excellent stimulant for a discussion of American history or what we may call the American experience. The shots that Braverman has included in his film were not simply selected at random. They were carefully chosen for the significant social forces they picture that have shaped our present day world.

An American Time Capsule can also be used as an introduction to an awareness of violence. The film is preeminently an explosion of change. We see compressed into a few minutes time the clash and strife of social evolution. How this ever accelerating tumult is brought about by living together in an ever expanding society is a question that the film suggests could be explored.

Finally, the film is a fascinating exercise in sensory perception. Most of the images appear on the screen only for fractions of seconds. Yet, we perceive them clearly and almost instantly make associations with other images on the screen and in our memories. We also place values on the meanings of the images. This whole complicated phenomenon of what we are able to see and what we think of what we see is an area that can be the subject of much fruitful discussion.

3 minutes—color
Rental—$10.00 (#16)
Purchase—$60.00 (#16)

Suggestions for the Use of
AN AMERICAN TIME CAPSULE

1: An interesting device here would be to screen the film without its soundtrack and have the audience beat out a rhythm in response to the picture track.

2: Make a montage of still photographs that parallel the development of the film or develop a whole new theme entirely. A montage in this context means a series of still photographs that when viewed in sequence develop a theme or a story line.

3: Screen the film first without the sound and then again with the soundtrack. What are the differences, in one sentence each, that each member of the audience has noticed between the two screenings?

DOES ANYONE HAVE TIME TO THINK?
Does anyone have time to think? Does the president have time to think? The daily calendar of the American president, with its endless appointments and glad-handing chores, not only excludes sustained thought but creates the kind of staccato, jangling pattern of mental activity that

leads to a demand for surcease rather than study.

If the president has no time to think, then who has? Almost everyone in Washington is spending so much time being strategical that almost no one is being historical. There are so many movers and shakers that there is hardly any room for thinkers.

The paradox, of course, is that we are busy doing nothing. Never before has so much leisure time been available to so many. Leisure hours now exceed working hours. But we have a genius for cluttering. We have somehow managed to persuade ourselves that we are too busy to think, too busy to read, too busy to look back, too busy to look ahead, too busy to understand that all our wealth and all our power are not enough to safeguard our future unless there is also a real understanding of the danger that threatens us and how to meet it. Thus, being busy is more than merely a national passion; it is a national excuse.

Editorial from the Saturday Review
Sept. 18, 1971

THE ORANGE AND THE GREEN

The situation in Northern Ireland traces its roots back to the beginnings of modern history and yet is as contemporary and modern a problem as we have in the world today. The partitioning of a people by the power brokers of Western Europe has cost us dearly in blood in Asia and Africa, but it is ironic and tragic that it still festers uncured right in the supposed heartland of Western civilization.

The story of Northern Ireland is not simply a tale of Protestant against Catholic. It is more accurately a tale of cynical selfishness by the rich against the poor in which every weapon of subtle political oppression has been utilized to the fullest. *The Orange and the Green* presents us with the raw face of ignorant prejudice. It is a bleak picture of a people locked into what seems to be an inescapable cycle of despair whose only relief is to pour out their hatred on their neighbors.

The film is powerful in its topicality and fleshes out the headlines which are currently confronting us. It is also valuable in the picture it gives us of prejudice. We get a sense of distance from the prejudice with which we must deal in our American society and are therefore able to see more clearly the objective ugliness of its roots and consequences.

21 minutes—color
Rental—$12.75 (#12)
Purchase—$275.00 (#12)

Suggestions for the Use of
THE ORANGE AND THE GREEN

1: What is the point of view of the film? Does the film present one side as right and as having the cause of justice on their side or does it go deeper than that?

2: The problem with which the film deals is in a foreign country. Are any parallels able to be drawn with the situation the film presents and our own situation here at home? List the parallels that occur to you and analyze how they resemble the situation in America and how they differ?

3: How important is the economic situation in Northern Ireland in the causation of the problems of bigotry and hatred we see in the film? How important is the problem of education regarding the situation?

THE MOST HATED MAN IN NEW MEXICO

One thing that has become clear to those interested in social reform in the United States is that there is more than simply just a problem of poverty. It is more accurate and hence more effective to speak of the problem of poverties. The problem of not having a living wage in a northern ghetto has a different causal structure than poverty in Appalachia, and the problem of rural poverty in the Southwest for Mexican Americans is a problem almost unique in itself.

The Most Hated Man in New Mexico deals with the problems of the Mexican Americans through the person of Reises Lopez Tijerina a man who has risen to be a leader of his Mexican brothers. Reises is in some ways even more controversial than Cesar Chavez, if that can be imagined. Whatever be his motivations Reises is a product of his social situation. He is a direct result of the injustice that has oppressed his people.

The film is interesting because it gives us a personal insight into a severe social ill that is afflicting our society. It can be used as part of a series that concentrates on poverty as a good introduction to one of the "poverties" of the U.S., or it can be utilized as a starting point for a discussion of one consequence of historical racism for which we are currently paying the price.

29 minutes—color
Rental—$15.00 (#12)
Purchase—$330.00 (#12)

91

Suggestions for the Use of
THE MOST HATED MAN IN NEW MEXICO

1: The historical problems regarding the Mexican Americans in the United States are in many ways unique. The film could be used as an introduction to a topical study of those problems. What are its historical roots? For example, what are the similarities of the Mexican American problem to the difficulties that American Indians are currently facing? How does the question of racism influence the problem? What role did economics play in the situation of the people we see in the film?

2: If this film were shown as part of a program with *The Orange and the Green* and/or *The Young Uns,* a many faceted discussion could be stimulated by concentrating on the similarities of the problems involved as well as the differences.

3: The technique of the film is also important especially in a film dealing with a social issue. What viewpoint does the film take towards the issues and the personalities that are presented in the film? How does the film get this viewpoint across? Who speaks in the film, in what context? Are the speaker's viewpoints backed up by the visual material we see in the film or contradicted? What shots do we see in the film, and in what order or sequence do we see them? How is sound used in the film: voices, music and sound effects? What image or sequence of images do you think are the most effective in the film? Why?

THE ANDERSON PLATOON

This is an excellent film done originally for French television. It takes its title from the name of the Lieutenant who commands the platoon the film follows for a few weeks of combat in Vietnam. The film is an excellent example of what has come to be known in film making as *cinema verite.* The major aspect of this style is that an attempt is made simply to follow the subjects of the film without interference or direction by the film maker throughout their daily existence. Other examples in this book would be the two films by Arthur Barron, *Death* and *Factory.*

The effect of following the platoon through their dangerous existence in Vietnam with a camera and a tape recorder is in some ways surprising. There are scenes of tension and excitement, especially one of an actual helicopter crash, but the overall effect of this recording of men in combat is really much more prosaic. The real horror of war is its deadening boredom and dullness. The men slog through jungle terrain constantly aware that they are in danger but also constantly harassed by the mud and bugs and the constant damp discomfort of their surroundings.

The battle we see is real as are the wounds that the men receive. But there is no thrill of the fight here. It is all a routine business that breeds a dogged fatalism in the men in the platoon and in the audience who shares their experience. The film, though, is not a boring experience but actually a strongly moving one. It does not strive for dramatic effects that are not part of the actual experience of the men it is filming. Also it does not, surprisingly enough, take an obvious point of view on its subject matter. It is more interested in allowing its subject to speak for itself. The result is that *The Anderson Platoon* is an eminently worthwhile and compassionate record of the experience of men in combat.

65 minutes—B&W
Rental—$50.00 (#6)
Purchase—$450.00 (#6)

Suggestions for the Use of
THE ANDERSON PLATOON

1: *The Anderson Platoon* would fit very well into any film seminar or program on the theme of war and peace. It is a vital and honest piece of film making and an extremely valid human document. The questions it raises about warfare are often not mentioned in the face of more dramatic issues. The most obvious issue that the film presents is the criminal waste of valuable time that war imposes on men who could be doing something much more interesting and valuable with their lives. War like most manifestations of evil is really boring and unexciting.

2: The film's style is also a valuable aspect for discussion. The *cinema verite* style which the film uses is an interesting one that could be profitably analyzed. How does the film maker introduce his subject? What shots does he select and in what order does he use them to get his viewpoint across? What do we hear on the soundtrack? What voices? What music (if any)? What sound effects?

GENERALS, COLONELS AND VIETNAM

The command mess for generals and selected colonels at Long Binh is an ultra-plush restaurant with an ample bar that could rival many first-class night spots in the States. The service certainly exceeds anything in the States. Vietnamese girls in traditional dress are waitresses, and enlisted men in white shirts and ties serve as bartenders and busboys— keeping glasses full of wine and passing out cigars on a silver platter after dinner.

A senior sergeant spent his time between Long Binh and Saigon making sure there was an ample supply of steak, lobster and booze. There were always more meals than needed in case a stray general dropped in.
Mark Jury

THE SELLING OF THE PENTAGON

This is the CBS documentary, which caused so much controversy when it was broadcast twice last year during prime time. It is a highly interesting film both for its subject matter and for the way it was presented.

The subject of the film is a report on the way the Defense Department spends a large part of its budget for self promotion. Everything from training and propaganda films to fun and games weekends where businessmen play guns with the real thing is shown to be part of the complex program of the public relations program for the military. The film examines all these elements and tries to explore more deeply the ramifications for our society. One of the major difficulties that is brought out is the fragile delicacy of the thin line between public relations and the influencing of national policy that appears to be subsidized by a department of government that is required by law to be apolitical.

The probing style of the film and the visual reports on which it relies to make its point make *The Selling of the Pentagon* a documentary film on our society that deserves serious consideration.

The film also contains a regretful section of film journalism, the validity of which caused a great deal of the controversy surrounding the film. There is an interview in the film by Roger Mudd of a high ranking Defense Department official. This official's answer to one of Mudd's questions is so edited that he appears to be answering another question. CBS claims that this device did not alter the information presented in any significant manner. The whole matter, though, did raise the question of the credibility of the news media.

Despite this lapse of judgment by CBS, the film as a whole is a telling one and brings up some interesting and provocative questions about the nature of our society and its value system.

52 minutes—color
Rental—$25.00 (#3, #16)

Suggestions for the Use of
THE SELLING OF THE PENTAGON

1: The film could most profitably be used not as a weapon of attack against the military but as an excellent introduction into the nature and scope of propaganda in our society. What the film really does is give a chilling picture of how our attitudes and beliefs can be subtly influenced by various kinds of media. The most obvious examples of this are the film clips we see from films that are still getting a great play, which almost call for a holy war against international communism. The dan-

ger of oversimplifying such a complex problem becomes chillingly real in a world that has so much naked power for self destruction.

2: The film obviously would fit into any discussion of peace. It could be profitably shown with *The Anderson Platoon* or *The Day Jack Pittman Died* in a film series on the subject of peace and war. It would also provide a contrast to such films as *The Magician, The Pistol, The Desert,* and *A Passing Phase.* These films treat the subject of human aggression from a more figurative point of view. Their technique and content could be profitably compared and contrasted.

LOVE

Love it not an easy or altogether natural condition.
It is always a struggle.

IT'S ABOUT THIS CARPENTER

A student film made at New York University, *It's About This Carpenter* lends itself to a wide variety of interpretations. This format of the film is a simple one. It merely follows a man on his journey from his Greenwich Village apartment through New York City to an uptown church. The dramatic and visual center of the film is that the man is carrying a huge wooden cross. This clever dramatic device involves the man and the city he is traversing in a whole new series of relationships. Is the man simply a carpenter delivering his wares to a customer, or does the film mean more than that?

The film is notable in its restrained use of the strong imagery that is inherent in the situation. A man carrying a huge wooden cross through a city could be played to the hilt for its symbolism. The strength of *It's About This Carpenter* is that it maintains its narrative simplicity while allowing for a host of relationships and new meanings to be seen by the audience.

14 minutes—B&W
Rental—$7.00 (#13)
Purchase—$85.00 (#13)

Suggestions for the Use of
IT'S ABOUT THIS CARPENTER

1: The film can be most obviously used in any discussion of the problem of God in our contemporary society. The carpenter encounters many different situations as he makes his journey across the city. Each event is significant on many levels, all of which could be discussed.

2: The film is really a simple one technically. The shots that the film maker has chosen and the way in which he has put them together could be carefully studied to see how they form the final whole.

OUPA

On first viewing *Oupa* is simply a film about belly dancers. It is made in the *cinema verite* style, a form of film making which attempts to allow the subjects of the film to tell their own story through their words and actions. We see them at work in some restaurants in New York and follow them throughout some other aspects of their lives. In short we get into the whole atmosphere of their daily lives.

The film is interesting because it presents not just belly dancers at work but a whole attitude towards women and their role in society. There is one whole sequence devoted to showing us one of the dancers teaching her skills to a group of housewives. We observe the class and listen to the comments of the teacher as she muses on why her pupils are going through the long and arduous process.

The film stands by itself as a well worked piece of cinematic art. It also allows us, however, to reflect on many of the values that it presupposes.

14 minutes—B&W
Rental—$9.50 (#13)

Suggestions for the Use of
OUPA

1: *Oupa* would very profitably be used in a film seminar that was studying the *cinema verite* film style. *Factory* and *Death* would be other examples that could be used to round

out the basis for a discussion. In this style of film making the film maker is ostensibly showing us simply what is happening without any interference from a director or writer. Yet good *cinema verite* has a definite structure and dramatic impact. What the film maker chooses to shoot in the first place, in what order he puts it together, and the use he makes of the soundtrack all are important questions that could be discussed.

2: Without becoming moralistic and puritanical the film could be discussed on the level of its social implications. What role are the women in the film expected to play? Would Gloria Steinem or Betty Freidan enjoy the film?

3: If there is a mixed audience, have them make a list of characteristics of the typical female stereotype. Make this list before the film. Have them make another after the film. Compare the two lists, male and female before and after. Did the film support or refute the stereotypes?

THE PROBLEM THAT HAS NO NAME

The problem lay buried, unspoken, for many years in the minds of American women. It was a strange stirring, a sense of dissatisfaction, a yearning that women suffered in the middle of the twentieth century in the United States. Each suburban wife struggled with it alone. As she made the beds, shopped for groceries, matched slipcover material, ate peanut butter sandwiches with her children, chauffeured Cub Scouts and Brownies, lay beside her husband at night—she was afraid to ask even of herself the silent question—"Is this all?"

For over fifteen years there was no word of this yearning in the millions of words written about women, for women, in all the columns, books and articles by experts telling women their role was to seek fulfillment as wives and mothers. Over and over women heard in voices of tradition and of Freudian sophistication that they could desire no greater destiny than to glory in their own femininity. Experts told them how to catch a man and keep him, how to breastfeed children and handle their toilet training, how to cope with sibling rivalry and adolescent rebellion; how to buy a dishwasher, bake bread, cook gourmet snails, and build a swimming pool with their own hands; how to dress, look, and act more feminine and make marriage more exciting; how to keep their husbands from dying young and their sons from growing into delinquents. They were taught to pity the neurotic, unfeminine, unhappy women who wanted to be poets or

*physicists or presidents. They learned that truly feminine women
do not want careers, higher education, political rights—the
independence and the opportunities that the old-fashioned
feminists fought for. Some women, in their forties and fifties,
still remembered painfully giving up those dreams, but most of
the younger women no longer even thought about them. A
thousand expert voices applauded their femininity, their
adjustment, their new maturity. All they had to do was devote
their lives from earliest girlhood to finding a husband and
bearing children.*
Betty Friedan

SURVIVAL WITH STYLE

This film is almost more a celebration than a
narrative film. Its central core is the Mary Day celebration that
had been celebrated at Immaculata College in Los Angeles. The
film draws its beauty from the contributions of two artists that
are central to the film. The first is the personality of Rita Kent,
formerly Sister Corita, whose influence and spirit are felt throughout the film. The other is Haskell Wexler, a leading Hollywood
cinematographer, whose creative personality from his position
behind the camera is constantly felt throughout the film.

What the film tries to do is to recapture the
atmosphere of the learning experience that occurs at Immaculata.
This spirit is felt in all aspects of the daily life there. We share
the mind of one of the faculty members, follow the students
through their work in a biology lab, and, finally, participate in
the Mary Day celebration.

The film is photographed with a touch of unique
genius the memory of which remains long after individual scenes
have been forgotten. We are able to enter into the singular
experience that was Immaculata, and yet at the same time
deeply feel the mystery of what it means to be alive.

27 minutes—color
Rental—$15.00 (#17)

Suggestions for the Use of
SURVIVAL WITH STYLE

1: Since this is such a well made film, it is a very

profitable one to analyze cinematically. Divide the film into sequences after the first screening. A sequence is more or less a unified section of the film that might form a separate episode. In this film the sequences could be divided according to the rough physical location in which they take place. There is nothing absolute about this division, and it shouldn't take too much time. After the division into sequences have various groups of the audience study the type and order of the shots in each sequence. What new information is provided by each shot? How is this information provided, by the visual material, by the soundtrack, by the order of the shots? There is no need to be extremely detailed here. One sentence per shot will do. After this is done for each sequence, have each group read their findings aloud matching the order of the sequences in the film.

2: A simple method of doing roughly the same thing is to have each member of the audience write a list of nouns modified by one adjective that describes their impression as the film is being screened. This is best done on the second showing of the film.

I'LL NEVER GET HER BACK

The agony of a young girl who must give her child up for adoption is the subject of this film. The format of the film is the reconstruction of the young girl's experience from her arrival at the home for unwed mothers to her final signing of the adoption papers. The soundtrack consists mainly of the girl's reflections on the painful experience she has undergone.

I'll Never Get Her Back is a simple film, which respects the human qualities of the girl involved in the critical dilemma she has to face. The film avoids the pitfalls of being either sensational or moralistic. Its quiet tone allows the hurt humanity of the girl to speak most eloquently for itself.

24 minutes—B&W
Rental—$10.00 (#12)
Purchase—$205.00 (#12)

Suggestions for the Use of
I'LL NEVER GET HER BACK

1: The subject matter of the film might prove to be
too particular for most film discussion situations. However, since
it is so well done, it might prove useful as a starting point for
a discussion of the question of moral choice. What processes must
the girl go through to come to her decision? What are the pressures
of society she must face? Are these pressures changing? What
other elements enter into her decision?

2: The subject matter of the film is a difficult one
to handle from the film makers point of view. What do you
think of the manner in which the film makers handled their
assignment here?

IF THERE WERE NO BLACKS

Set in a cemetery with a group of characters who
are a variety of social types *If There Were No Blacks* is a
powerful yet often comic morality play which is as contemporary
as this morning's newspaper. The film is cleverly written with a
touch of humorous surrealism that manages to keep our interest
throughout.

The plot of the film, such as it is, concerns a young
man who enters the cemetery desperately wanting to be
accepted by the society he finds there. The main difficulty he
meets is the refusal of a blind man to believe that he is not black.
The absurd situation of stubborn rejection gradually develops
until it involves all the characters in the graveyard. The main
thrust of the film revolves around the reactions of the other
people in the graveyard to the plight of the young man, who is
gradually cracking up under the pressure of social ostracism.

We meet a paranoid army officer, a young liberal
doctor, a bourgeoise undertaker, a judge, and a poor sexton.
Their characterization is more as types than as fully rounded
personalities, but the force of the film comes from the crystal
clear presentation of their irrationality. The selfish absurdity of
most human motivations with all the mixtures of fear, greed, and
hypocrisy is presented as chillingly real.

If There Were No Blacks probes the often ugly side
of the wide variety of human relationships that goes into making

up a civilization. It is a very serious film about some very serious questions. The skill of the film's creators is brought out by the clever balance of humor and seriousness that pervades the whole work. We find ourselves laughing constantly, yet always involved with what is happening on the screen.

58 minutes—B&W
Rental—$30.00 (#11)
Purchase—$330.00 (#11)

Suggestions for the Use of
IF THERE WERE NO BLACKS

1: This film should provide no difficulty for discussion. The only problem that might arise is keeping the discussion going along one line. One suggestion would be to have a character analysis of each of the main characters in the film. What do they represent? How are they typical or untypical of the class in society they are supposed to represent?

2: The film uses a slightly surrealistic technique. What does surreal mean in the context of the play? How does it get its point across? Would the film have been more effective if it had been done more traditionally, i.e., by not making the characters so comically absurd?

THE REVOLUTIONARY IMPULSE
When the revolutionary impulse to strike out against the oppressor is stifled, distortions in the personality appear. During the Algerian Revolution, Fanon worked in a hospital in Algeria. A psychiatrist, there he was able to observe carefully Algerians who had caved in psychologically under the pressures of a revolutionary situation. The Wretched of the Earth contains an appendix in which Fanon introduces several of these case histories, tracing the revolutionary impulse and attempts to evade it through the psyches of his patients.
Not all of Fanon's patients were Algerian colonial subjects. French policemen who were bothered by the brutality with which they were surrounded and in which they were involved, French soldiers who had inflicted despicable tortures on prisoners, were often confronted with situations in which their rationalizations broke down and they found themselves face to face with their own merciless deeds.
Eldridge Cleaver

107

THE PARTY

The Party is a dramatization of some of the problems of sexual intimacy and human growth. Three teenage couples, who have had varying degrees of sexual relationships, borrow a beach house for a weekend. The action of the film centers on the first evening when they arrive and start to feel the place out. The dramatic and psychological interaction in the film involves all three couples and penetrates below the surface in its exploration of human relationships and motivations.

The role of peer group pressure comes to the fore with its concomitant effect of the blunting of human sensibilities. Attitudes reflecting a variety of personal pressures are brought out in the personal interaction of the three couples. The main thrust of the film is to bring out that the nature of a sexual relationship involves the total person in all its complexity.

28 minutes
Rental—$17.95 color (#1)
    —$11.95 B&W (#1)
Purchase—$270.00 color (#14)
    —$135.00 B&W (#14)

Suggestions for the Use of
THE PARTY

1: *The Party* is one of the films from the *Insight* series which specifically attempts to deal with a variety of human problems. As such the film is specifically geared to provoke a discussion of the problem it explores. *The Party* could be profitably used to fit into any discussion of the complexity of the problem of maturing both socially and sexually. In this day and age of the growing awareness of personal responsibility the film covers the subject it treats with intelligence and sensitivity.

BEHOLD . . . ALL THINGS NEW

The World Council of Churches met at Upsala, Sweden in 1968. *Behold . . . All Things New,* a film produced by Swedish television for the occasion, is an attempt to get at the heart of what this meeting, and, indeed all religion, is all about.

The film is a stream of consciousness journey through the world events of today that are part and parcel of the fears and aspirations of contemporary man. We see the maelstrom of today's world flowing before us and hear the voices of men attempting to relate Christianity to the seemingly unstructured flow of human history.

The double edged risk of trying to live a committed Christian life is always felt hovering in the background. On the one hand there is the danger of smug contentment; on the other the trap of cynical despair. The theme of the film, though, is always realistically hopeful, and it thankfully refrains from any attempt at neat answers.

27 minutes—color
Rental—$20.00 (#11)
Purchase—$245.00 (#11)

Suggestions for the Use of
BEHOLD . . . ALL THINGS NEW

1: This film is most obviously useful in some specifically religious context, although not exclusively so. It contains a wealth of material that asks to be discussed. Everything from the most theoretical questions of philosophy and purpose of organized

109

religion to the most concrete and practical problems facing us every day are evoked by a viewing of the film. It is an excellent discussion starter.

2: The film covers a great deal of time and space in its varied presentation. It is somewhat of a film collage. Make a collection of still photographs that could substitute for the various scenes that are seen in the film. Why have the film makers chosen the shots they have? How does their choice compare to yours?

SPEND IT ALL

The French speaking Cajun people of Louisiana's bayou country and their music flow through this beautiful and lyrical film. The Cajuns in the American south are the descendants of the original immigrants who were forced to flee from Canada in the 18th century. The film is a significantly beautiful portrait of this unique pocket of American culture.

Spend It All like *The Blues Accordin' to Lightnin' Hopkins* explores the music of a people and its intimate ties to their lifestyle. It constantly presents some aspect of Cajun life and then flows into a natural summation of the whole atmosphere of what we have just seen with a musical coda. Dewey Balfa,

Nathan Abshire, Adam Landrenau, Marc Savoy, Cajun names that are as unique as the music they get out of their fiddles and accordions.

The film is valuable as an introduction into the lives of a little explored part of American culture. It is at the same time a singularly beautiful art work in itself. The film maker, Les Blank, the same man who did *Blues Accordin' to Lightnin' Hopkins,* studiously avoids cinematic tricks in composing his film. His camera work is subtly unobtrusive, yet it constantly presents us with a vitally gripping series of visual images.

41 minutes—color
Rental—$60.00 (#9)
Purchase—$500.00 (#9)

Suggestions for the Use of
SPEND IT ALL

1: The film is a beautiful example of musical ethnography. It brings to us in a visually fascinating forty one minutes a picture of the natural flow of a people's music from their daily lives. We feel at the end of the film that we have spent some time not as tourists but as participants in the Cajun life. *Spend It All* would fit in perfectly in a film festival that had the family of man or some similar theme as its emphasis. It would also be an excellent film to include in a film series dedicated to music.

2: Since the film is a bit more expensive than most of the others mentioned in this book, *Spend It All* should be used for special occasions where the most benefit can be gained from it. It should be shown as the highlight of a particular occasion such as an assembly of students or festival devoted to American music.

3: The film could also be employed as part of an ethnographic film festival, i.e., a screening of films that try to show the variety of life styles in our contemporary world. *Dead Birds, The Ballad of the Crowfoot, Ishi in Two Worlds,* and Les Blank's other film, *The Blues Accordin' to Lightnin' Hopkins* would make a powerful film festival.

THE COMPOSER
One of the first things most people want to hear discussed in relation to composing is the question of inspiration.

They find it difficult to believe that composers are not as preoccupied with that question as they had supposed. The layman always finds it hard to realize how natural it is for the composer to compose. He has a tendency to put himself into the position of the composer and to visualize the problems involved, including that of inspiration, from the perspective of the layman. He forgets that composing to a composer is like fulfilling a natural function. It is like eating or sleeping. It is something that the composer happens to have been born to do; and, because of that, it loses the character of a special virtue in the composer's eyes.

Aaron Copeland

NOT ME ALONE

A thirty minute color film about natural childbirth, *Not Me Alone* is a simple, straightforward film document about an aspect of human love. The format of the film is to follow an expectant couple through the process of preparation for the birth and then through the actual birth itself. The film attempts to be as objective and as informational as possible allowing the innate drama of the event to speak for itself.

30 minutes—color
Rental—$30.00 (#15)
Purchase—$275.00 (#15)

Suggestions for the Use of
NOT ME ALONE

1: *Not Me Alone* **is primarily an informational film. It attempts to document a vital human process. Despite its simplicity, however, it also manages to capture the multileveled human drama that is taking place. The subtle relationships between the parents themselves, between the parents and their child, and between the doctors and nurses involved are obviously there, although not overly dramatized. The film, then, can be put to good use on a simple informational level. It is a clear and respectful presentation of fact.**

2: *Not Me Alone* **can also be included with profit in a series of films that deal with various aspects of human**

relationships. It is above all a human document that captures on film a great deal of the total meaning of human love.

ONE NEETAH AND MICKEY

This is an experimental film by Michael Siporin, an independent film maker working in New York. In *One Neetah and Mickey* he has composed a filmic triptych, an autobiographical portrait of himself, his wife Juanita, and the subtle nuances of their relationship. The film also explores the latent artistic possibilities of a number of different film stocks or types with a variety of camera techniques throughout its three parts. There is also a tension between the visual elements we see on the screen, i.e., the style and manner in which they are photographed, and the mystery of their personalities which we see developed in the film. Who are they? What do they think and feel? What is the secret of their relationship?

The first part of the film is a portrait of Mike. We see him in his studio as he goes through the motions of sitting in his chair. This simple action is repeated several times with minor variations in camera position as he looks into the camera. His expression is serious, almost somber, and the slow rhythm of the shots enhances the mood. Then subtly the mood shifts. The pace of the shots quickens as we see a series of single frame

113

comic mug shots superimposed on the slower, more reflective sequences. The complexity of the image matches the complexity of the personality portrayed.

The second section, the portrait of Juanita is photographed with high contrast film. No shadows appear, only stark black and white. The effect is startling, and the visual analogy that comes to mind is a charcoal portrait set to motion.

The final part of the triptych deals with Mike and Juanita together. This section is shot in color, and its effect is heightened by the culmination of the techniques used in the previous two sections. The film is a remarkable balance of the affective personality of the film maker and his creative intelligence. His personal statement is tightly controlled by his sensitivity to form, rhythm, and texture.

7 minutes—color/B&W
Rental—$15.00 (#4, #7)

Suggestions for the Use of
ONE NEETAH AND MICKEY

1: This is a fairly sophisticated film and the experimental technique in the film might not be suitable for profitable use in a group that sees films only occasionally. It can be used with great profit with a group who are relatively used to seeing films and want to explore the new uses to which the film medium can be put. The film is very subtle in its presentation of the mystery of the human personality and is an extremely beautiful visual film to view.

2: *One Neetah and Mickey* would be an excellent addition to a program of experimental films. *Starlight*, and the other film by Michael Siporin, *Bang Head, Go Bang, Bang* also would fit very well into such a program. The film would also provide excellent variety in a program of films dealing more or less explicitly with human relationships. *Not Me Alone, The Break, The Couple*, and *In the Kitchen* would make for a good mini film festival of high artistic quality.

THE WRITER
One of the real problems in writing, whether its fiction or nonfiction, is to have one's head in the clouds but your feet on the earth. So in a theoretical essay, you are sometimes carried away by a purely abstract flight of thought. Now, bisociation

114

*means in this context that you suddenly say to yourself, "Well,
I'm talking about real people, about real down-to-earth reality."
Then you bring in an illustration of your abstract idea which
pulls you down to reality. Metaphors, realistic metaphors. Or, in
fiction writing, you work on a dialog, or a description of something,
and suddenly you say, "Well, this is here and now, and this
person is here and now," and put your nose into it. A train of
thoughts moves under its own inertia, you know, as a body set in
motion goes on moving. But when you manage to catch yourself,
to realize that you are up on a flight, and then manage to pull
it down to earth, well that's bisociation.*
Arthur Koestler

A WELL SPENT LIFE

"If your mule dies, buy another. If your nigger dies,
hire another."

Mance Lipscomb is 75 years old, black, a former
sharecropper in Texas, and one of the greatest guitarists in the
world. *A Well Spent Life* is a portrait of Mance Lipscomb, his
life, his music, and his people. The beauty of the film flows
from the sensitivity of the film maker, Les Blank, to the essence
of the life of this black Texas sharecropper. We are there,
physically and spiritually, are baptized in the river, keep time at

the dance hall, and listen to the music and the words of the man that is Mance Lipscomb.

A Well Spent Life like *Blues Accordin' to Lightnin' Hopkins* and *Spend It All* is a film that has that elusive quality called presence. They are many films about people, valid film records of life styles and sufferings. There are far fewer films that are with people, films that bring us beyond the sights and sounds we sense on the screen to a real sense of oneness with the people we see in the film. *A Well Spent Life* is such a film.

44 minutes—color
Rental—$60.00 (#9)
Purchase—$535.00 (#9)

Suggestions for the Use of
A WELL SPENT LIFE

1: This is an excellent human document both on a man and on his music. It is not to be missed in any group that is dealing with music, especially the roots of American blues.

2: *A Well Spent Life* can stand by itself as a film that would bear a close analysis into its makeup. The film gets us right into the life of its subject. How does it do this? What use does the film maker make of the soundtrack? How does this blend with the material we see on the screen? What kind of shots does the film contain, close ups, wide shots? How long are they on the screen? Are there short shots, i.e., a few seconds, or longer, more meditative shots? In what order do they occur on the screen?

PAS DE DEUX

Pas De Deux is a film by Norman McClaren, a master of visual experimentation in film making. In this film he complements with the artistic resources of the film medium the beauty of the dance. The basic device he uses in this film is a multi-imaged effect by the clever use of an optical printer. The successive movement of the dancers is reprinted several times on the same frame of the film. The final effect is that the progressing movement of the dancer's bodies are seen like footprints through the snow. We see a hand move from point A

116

to point B while at the same time seeing its traces throughout the whole sequence.

The film is not just an exercise in technical highjinx. It is a lyric visual commentary on the beauty of movement.

14 minutes—B&W
Rental—$12.00 (#16)
Purchase—$100.00 (#16)

Suggestions for the Use of
PAS DE DEUX

1: This film can be used as a simple demonstration of the unique powers of film to present reality. The dance we see is a beautiful art form in itself, but it is skillfully enhanced by the film's singular technique. *Pas De Deux* **would make up an excellent program of lyrical films if it were to be screened with** *Starlight, Turned On, Moods of Surfing, One Neetah and Mickey,* **and** *Dream of the Wild Horses.* **These films communicate a great deal, but their means of communication are more poetic and suggestive than intellectually definable. What is communicated in each of these films? How does the film maker make use of his visual material? How does he photograph it? In what lighting situations? From what angle or physical point of view?**

What use does he make of the soundtrack? Does he emphasize voice or sound effects? Do the sounds we hear naturally flow from the pictures we see on the screen or do they act as a contrast to the visual material? In what order do things happen in the film? What pictures follow what pictures? What sounds follow what sounds?

THE COUPLE

The Couple is like *The Break* the work of a student film maker attempting to do something new with the medium. It is a subtle film that suggests rather than definitively outlines the struggles of a young married couple to make their relationship work. The methodology of the film is to use significant places as the motif for the story. The first thing we see in the film is a bare apartment. Noises and then voices off camera introduce a young couple who we guess are inspecting it with an eye to renting it. The camera work here at the beginning of the film sets the relationship between the audience and the characters in the film. We are never allowed to get too close to them. Indeed we seem to be closer to the walls and ceilings of the apartment than we do to them. It is as though we are looking at the couple with the same cool detachment as the walls and ceilings of the rooms they are living in.

The stages of the couple's relationship are deftly suggested with a careful selection of shots that reveal subtle clues to their ongoing psychological moods. The motivation for these moods is not provided as we follow them through the early days of their marriage in the apartment. I suspect that there is a method in the film maker's madness here though. By concentrating on the motif of the apartment and by not allowing us to get too close to this particular couple, I think that he is pointing to something else. This something else really cannot be reduced to a simple description in words the same way a poem cannot be reduced to a formula. I feel, however, that the film maker here is saying something about the human condition. Love is not an easy or an altogether natural condition. It is always a struggle. In this film the apartment is the given element. It remains stolidly the same, almost unaffected by time and life. The struggle it contains in this film, we suspect will be acted out again and again, always new and always difficult.

15 minutes—B&W
Rental—$8.00 (#13)
Purchase—$75.00 (#13)

Suggestions for the Use of
THE COUPLE

1: Make a shot list of the film or at least part of it.
A shot list is a description of each separate shot in the sequence
of a film. Make a note of the information or visual material
you see in each shot. Now the important part. How does the
film maker create his film with putting these individual parts
together? Put yourself in the film maker's place and try to
rearrange the shots to tell the story.

THE WAR OF THE EGGS

This brief dramatic film reveals the process of self-
discovery of a young couple who are forced to face themselves
when their young child is injured after a family argument. They
reveal themselves as they wait in the anteroom of the hospital
where their child is being treated. The dialog is skillfully written
so as to allow us to share in their process of self-discovery.

The obvious problem of the film is that their marriage simply isn't working. The injury to their child is only the final manifestation of their inner pain. As the film develops we begin to share more and more of the couple's suffering. Their exterior defenses slowly break down before us, and we are able to enter more and more deeply into their psyches. Most importantly, perhaps, is that we are able to see their problems as also in some way very close to our own.

The film intelligently stops short of supplying a pat answer to the difficulties it presents. It leaves the couple and the audience at the critical point of decisive action.

28 minutes
Rental—$17.95 color (#1)
  —$11.95 B&W (#1)
Purchase—$270.00 color (#14)
  —$135.00 B&W (#14)

Suggestions for the Use of
THE WAR OF THE EGGS

1: The subject of the film is the problem of self-acceptance. It makes the point that we are unable to relate to others happily unless first we are able to accept ourselves. More and more the idea of being fully human is seen as being impossible without living in community. The definition of being a man is now being drawn not from abstract essence, but more from the nature and extent of human relationships. *The War of the Eggs* provides a base for the discussion of this question of self-acceptance and interpersonal communication.

2: This film is similar to both *The Couple* and *The Break* in basic subject matter but extremely different in purpose and technique. The three films would make for an excellent seminar on human communication. The three films all have a definite point of view, and the similarities and differences between each film could be discussed with profit. For example, the dialog in *The War of the Eggs* is essential to the film. In the other two films there is no dialog at all. How this affects the film's relative content and effect on the audience is an interesting question.

THREE BY ROBERT FLAHERTY:
NANOOK OF THE NORTH,
MAN OF ARAN,
LOUISIANA STORY

The genius of Robert Flaherty is a film experience that simply should not be missed. He was an American film maker of such unique talent that his name is known today as synonomous with what has become to be known as the documentary film. Flaherty was an artist devoted to his art. His predominant passion was to celebrate the beauty of man over and against the elements. He would spare no pain or hardship to transport himself and his primitive portable motion picture equipment to some of the most difficult areas of the earth in order to capture the concrete manifestations of his theme, man versus nature. What has resulted from his efforts are films that transcend the natural fascination of the exotic locations he used. They are simple masterpieces, perfect blends of form and content that are a marvel to behold.

Nanook of the North is a first-rate presentation of the basic elements of Eskimo life. It is not just another travelogue to the land of the igloos, but captures the raw courage of men in a style that has yet to be equalled.

Man of Aran is a film of the fishermen of Western Ireland, whom John Millington Synge found so fascinating in *Riders to the Sea*. They are a tough breed of men whose daily

121

struggles with the North Atlantic Flaherty immortalizes on film.

In *Louisiana Story* there is a quieter, more bucolic mood. Flaherty attempts here to show how man can live with the advance of technology. Ostensibly the film deals with the incursion of a floating oil rig into the bayous of a Louisiana swamp. Really the film is a quiet and masterful presentation of the life of a boy and his family on the bayou. The film subtly involves us in the whole atmosphere of the life that is native to southern Louisiana. We are entranced by the quiet rhythms of the film that match perfectly the subdued pulse of the life style it presents.

Nanook of the North
55 minutes—B&W
Rental—$25.00 (#6)
Man of Aran
77 minutes—B&W
Rental—$50.00 (#6)
Louisiana Story
77 minutes—B&W
Rental—$50.00 (#6)

Suggestions for the Use of the FLAHERTY FILMS

1: It is difficult to pin these films down to any specific pedagogical usage. They are each so rich in content and beauty of expression, though, that they can't fail to cause discussions on everything from their subject matter to Flaherty's film making style. Each film bears a lode of raw material in the way that it was put together. Why does Flaherty use the shots that he gives us? Why does he keep them on the screen for the length of time that he does? How do they express a point of view about the subjects? What is that point of view?

2: Any or all of these films would make an excellent film festival addition. The three could be shown together or with such films as *Spend It All, Blues' Accordin' to Lightnin' Hopkins, The Anderson Platoon, Confrontation* and the other documentary style films shown in this book. The richness and variety of the human experience would be an overwhelmingly moving theme.

HAPPINESS

This generation is the first that can't take as its primary concern the age-old questions that have agitated all deep thinkers since civilization began.

THE SEARCHING EYE

This brief film essay on seeing is a minor masterpiece in the expressive use of the creative use of the film medium. Saul Bass, the film maker who also created *Why Man Creates,* has masterfully put together this precisely structured bit of cinema built around the theme of how man sees.

The film is based on our sharing the visual experiences of a small boy as he explores the world around him. His "seeing", and consequently ours, is not just limited to the physical but extends into his imagination as visual metaphors constantly suggest themselves to him. For example, the flight of some gulls suggests the attempts of man to imitate them, and we watch as the figure of man trying to fly is superimposed on the movement of the birds and finally a jet plane appears.

The film also explores what man has learned to see that is beyond the power of his naked eye. We go into the world of the microscope to experience the wonders of the tiny universes we rarely suspect exist. We see a crater on the moon and the eruption of a volcano. A time lapse sequence shows the growth of a plant capsulized into a few seconds.

The film is a technical marvel, but it is much more than a collection of cinematic tricks. What the film maker has done is to cleverly explore the range of one aspect of the possibilities of human experience. The film cannot fail but to hold its audience from beginning to end.

25 minutes—color
Rental—$15.00 (#16)
Purchase—$270.00 (#16)

Suggestions for the Use of
THE SEARCHING EYE

1: The value of this film for use as a discussion starter on anything from technology to poetry will immediately become evident upon screening it. The film maker's skillful inclusion of a wide variety of visual experiences is really meant to be the beginning of a further exploration not an end. The world of microscopy, biology and a host of other fields of study are brilliantly introduced in this film. Also there is a great deal of visual metaphor that illustrates the creative use of man's imagination. A good discussion question might simply be to explore the real implications of what and how man really sees. Is sight just a physical process or is it a much wider experience?

2: *The Searching Eye* would make an excellent companion film for Rolf Forsberg's film, *Awareness*. Forsberg also explores the question of man's seeing something, but his approach is entirely different than Bass's. Both films attempt to make us more sensitive to the world around us, but the artistic vision of the two film makers is really different. How they see their respective universes and how they present them to us would make for an interesting and illuminating discussion.

3: Cut one square inch out of a piece of cardboard or construction paper. Place the piece of paper with the hole cut from the center over a magazine or newspaper photograph and move it about the whole photograph. The hole in the cardboard should reveal only one square inch at a time of the whole photograph, and the eye will begin to perceive the interesting patterns that emerge. Write one sentence descriptions of the forms that emerge.

THE YOUNG UNS

The Young Uns is excellent in presenting a complex problem clearly and portraying the people involved in that problem as human beings and not just statistics. We see, first of all in the film, the fact that poverty is a complex social problem that in many cases has nothing to do with peoples' willingness to work. The Tablers are hard working to a fault and still are getting nowhere. Then the film shows us the beauty of the Tablers themselves. We see the daily activities of a young boy

who is left with the responsibility for the family sincerely trying to make a go of it despite what seem to be overwhelming odds. The courage of his spirit matches the hard beauty of the mountains in which he lives.

27 minutes—color
Rental—$15.00 (#12)
Purchase—$330.00 (#12)

Suggestions for the Use of
THE YOUNG UNS

1: This film is an ideal resource for a discussion on the complexities of poverty in the modern United States. What are some of these complexities as presented in the film? Is the poverty of the Tabler family a result of laziness, poor planning on their part or bad luck? In what sense can it be said that society has passed them by?

2: Have each member of the audience write a few sentences on what the specific problem is in the film. Read as many as possible aloud. How many basically agree? Disagree? What are the main points of agreement and disagreement?

3: Haye each member of the audience make a list of adjectives on the effects of poverty on the Tablers. How many of these adjectives really have to do with money?

ACCELERATION

Acceleration is an example of the excellent animation work coming out of Yugoslavia these days. It is a short ironic commentary on the restlessness of modern man, which is often mistaken for a virtue in itself. The history of man's scientific progress in a capsulized form is presented here with a strong satirical twist.

A primitive man lies drinking nectar from the tree of life. A sudden restlessness seizes him, and he determines to climb a nearby mountain. A number of makeshift devices fail to get him to his goal, until his manic drive leads him to build a spaceship with which he is able to reach the peak. The result of all his efforts is his discovery of another tree with the same nectar he had in the first place.

The point of the satire in the film is a subtle one. At first viewing it can be taken to be a condemnation of all progress, especially scientific. This position is really a misrepresentation of what the film is saying. More precisely the film is a commentary of the almost irrational desire of our Western world to see simple movement as an end in itself.

129

2 minutes—color
Rental—$5.00 (#11)
Purchase—$40.00 (#11)
This film can be rented with *Homo Homini* for $15.00 and sold
with it for $175.00.

Suggestions for the Use of
ACCELERATION

**1: Stop the film just before the launching of the
spaceship. Have each member of the audience write a sentence on
how the film will end. Screen the rest of the film and compare
the opinions of the audience as to the film's probable ending.
Take a vote on which one is the best ending, the actual one or
one of those written by the audience.**

**2: Is the film a pessimistic one? Why or why not?
Take a vote and have the voters explain their answers in short,
one sentence, if possible, answers.**

DEFENSE DEPARTMENT BUDGET, 1972
*With relatively little attention from the press and
even less from the public, Congress has approved a fiscal year
1972 Defense Department Budget of roughly $75 billion, give
or take a few billion. Included in this total is about $21 billion for
research, development, and procurement of a variety of military
hardware. Buried in all these figures is the comparatively trifling
sum of $370 million to start development engineering on the
B-1, the Air Force's new manned strategic bomber. Trifling or not,
this early funding represents only the tip of the iceberg. The
entire B-1 program may end up costing anywhere from $10 to
$50 billion, depending on who's doing the estimating.*
Berkeley Rice

HOMO HOMINI

There is an ever increasing pressure in our contemporary society to bow down to the all healing god of science.
This film is a protest against that pressure. Science as an answer
to all our problems tends to break down in the face of a
humanity that resists it as an all embracing value.

130

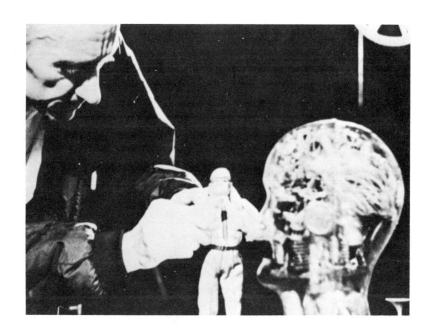

In *Homo Homini* we are presented with a brief animated satire as the ability of science to be a universal panacea. An efficient looking marionette replete with white shirt and tie and wearing horn rimmed glasses sits in front of an impressive looking if slightly grotesque computer. He coolly feeds information into the computer, the central feature of which is a transparent plastic skull. Massive human concerns are reduced to mathematical problems to be dealt with by the computer. The pace of the problems with which the machine is asked to deal gets faster and faster, as the huge apparatus tries to deal with all of humanity. Images of man's beauty flash through the man's mind as he scampers about trying to keep up the pace. These he quickly dismisses as useless distractions from his main task. They are simply not scientific enough.

Finally, the machine breaks down and collapses in a smoking hulk under the pressure of all that humanity. The scientist is left stranded amidst all that useless wreckage. Just then we see Rodin's statue, *The Thinker,* over his shoulder. This marvelous expression of the human soul is another aspect of humanity that refuses to be reduced to a number.

11 minutes—color
Rental—$12.50 (#11)
Purchase—$110.00 (#11)

1: What is the relationship between Isaac Asimov's point in the citation quoted and the film? What levels of progress are discussed in the film? In the Asimov quote?

2: Have each member of the audience make one word list as to what is important to him. This can be done anonymously. How many of these items can be solved by advancing technology? Discuss why and how they can or cannot be.

WHEN ARISTOTLE FAILS,
TRY SCIENCE FICTION
There is an accepted consensus in science and to be a plausible fake in science (before any audience not utterly ignorant in the field) one must learn that consensus thoroughly. Having learned it, however, one has no need to be a plausible fake.

In other fields of intellectual endeavor there is, however, no accepted consensus. The different schools argue endlessly, moving in circles about each other as fad succeeds fashion over the centuries. Though individuals may be unbelievably eloquent and sincere, there is, short of the rack and the stake, no decision ever. Consequently, to be a plausible fake in religion, art, politics, mysticism, or even any of the "soft" sciences such as sociology (to anyone not utterly expert in the field), one need only learn the vocabulary and develop a certain self-assurance . . .

This generation, then, is the first that can't take as its primary concern the age-old questions that have agitated all deep thinkers since civilization began. Those questions are still interesting, but they are no longer of the first importance, and any literature that deals with them (that is, any literature but science fiction) is increasingly irrelevant.
Isaac Asimov

DECORATION

This film is a clever little satire on "do-goodism." The point it makes is a subtle one, but it tells its story with broad strokes of black humor. *Decoration* is an animated short which presents us with a little man walking across an empty field. Suddenly a prone figure of a person, who presumably is sick, appears out of nowhere. Our hero reacts instinctively and carries the fallen man over the horizon to a hospital. He hurries back to us only to find another fallen figure on the ground. Once again our hero performs a truly humanitarian gesture and rushes him off to the hospital.

The process keeps repeating itself, but now we notice that our "do-gooder" has a new medal pinned to his chest every time he returns from the hospital. As more and more fallen people are rushed off to the hospital, more and more medals appear on his tunic. Finally, weighted down by the collection of human approval on his chest, our man collapses under their pressure and the medals become his own coffin. A group of clean up men then appear and cart the coffin to a machine which is constantly punching out a new collection of medals.

The force of this short film comes from its ironical commentary on human nature. It is an excellent antidote to any oversimplification of the question of human motivation, especially in relation to social causes.

7 minutes—color
Rental—$15.00 (#11)
Purchase—$135.00 (#11)

Suggestions for the Use of
DECORATION

1: *Decoration* **would be best seen in conjunction with a series of other films on social responsibility. As was mentioned above, it serves as an excellent check on the sometimes unwarranted enthusiasm that is generated by a discussion on human betterment.** *Decoration* **does not put down helping one's neighbor, but points out the duplicity of human motives.**

2: The film would also be an excellent addition to any film seminar on animated films. Other such films are *Chromophobia, Scabies, American Time Capsule,* **and** *A Note from Above.* **Such a seminar might concentrate on the varieties of technique involved in the making of these films, the common characteristics of how they get their points across, and the type or types of effects they have on their audiences.**

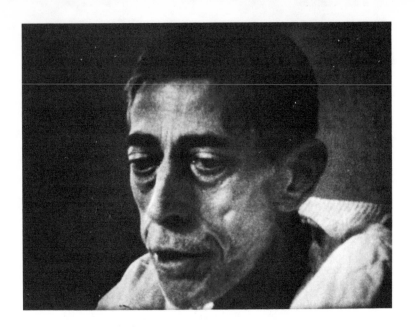

DEATH

This is a harsh film, perhaps the harshest of the films mentioned in this book. Arthur Barron, the film maker, simply obtained the permission of a man dying of cancer in a Catholic hospital in New York to film his last days. The resultant film is an unforgettable cinematic statement.

What Barron would claim that he is doing here is a straightforward job of photo-journalism, simply recording the harsh reality of a man's last days in a cancer ward. Relentlessly the camera follows the man and his fellow patients through their daily routine. We see the man wheeled around the hospital, a shrunken husk of his former self who can only think of the pain which is with him every waking moment. We see his sister and brother and his co-workers and hear their reactions to his imminent demise and their recollections of him as a person. We see his empty apartment and hear him reminisce about his life. Finally, we see him a few seconds after his death, as the nurses prepare his body to be removed for burial.

The film is almost machinelike in its attempt to render an objective account of its subject matter. The images we see on the screen, however, cry out for interpretation. The Mass we see and the hymn we hear at the beginning of the film, the visit of the priest to the patients, and the blank stares of the dying as they sit in a common room while a television drones on in the background unnoticed, all present us with a point of view about the reality of dying.

Death is not a pleasant film. Its stripping away of the social barriers we erect between ourselves and the unpleasant aspects of our human existence can be upsetting. It is an honest film, however, and it is this honesty that forces us to relate to its truth.

43 minutes—B&W
Rental—$35.00 (#8)
Purchase—$275.00 (#8)

Suggestions for the Use of DEATH

1: Have the audience write a list of gut reactions to the scenes in the film during its screening. Encourage them to write only one word that immediately comes to mind for each reaction. Have them read aloud after the screening of the film. Is there any rough consensus? Explore the common reactions. Is there a wide divergence in some of the words listed? Pursue these divergences.

2: The film is ostensibly a simple recording of a man going through his last days. Does the film seem to have a point of view in its presentation? Have the members of the audience write one sentence descriptions of what this point of view might be. If there is a consensus, what is it and how was it arrived at? What did the film maker do to express a point of view about death in the film? What shots did he use and in what order? What did he put on the soundtrack and with what picture?

3: Ask the members of the audience to write down the scene that affected them most strongly. Find out after the film whether there is a consensus here. Discuss why the shots which were picked were chosen.

SILENCE WHICH IS COMMUNICATION

Just as the most eager speaking at one another does not make a conversation (this is most clearly shown in that curious sport, aptly termed discussion, that is, "breaking apart," which is indulged in by men who are to some extent gifted with the ability to think), so for a conversation no sound is necessary, not even a gesture. Speech can renounce all the media of sense, and it is still speech.
Martin Buber

135

THE SUN'S GONNA SHINE

Les Blank is an independent film maker who has
made a number of beautiful documentary films that deal with the
musical folkways of America. *The Sun's Gonna Shine* is a short
film that deals with the same character as Blank's longer
treatment of the same man, *Blues Accordin' to Lightnin' Hopkins*.
I hesitate to call Blank's films documentary, because we usually
think of the documentary as a narrative form. *The Sun's Gonna
Shine* is really more analogous to a beautiful lyric poem in the
style in which it communicates.

The film deals with Lightnin' Hopkins, a blind, black
guitarist from the red clay country of West Texas. Les Blank
has composed his film from the visual images of Lightnin's home
country and the sound of Lightnin's guitar to tell the story of
the day when Lightnin' first decided to leave home and become
a wandering minstrel. The film is a beautiful bit of real film
making. Lightnin' and his neighbors are in tight economic
straights, and the film doesn't hide that fact. Despite this
deprivation the film brings out the singular beauty of the human
spirit. The music of Lightnin' Hopkins is born out of pain, but
it also affirms that *The Sun's Gonna Shine*.

The film can be viewed both as a singular work of
art and as a skilled portrait of a people.

10 minutes—color
Rental—$25.00 (#9)
Purchase—$125.00 (#9)

Suggestions for the Use of
THE SUN'S GONNA SHINE

1: This film would be well worth seeing just for the beautiful craftsmanship that it manifests. It is simply an excellent piece of film making. It can also be used in a discussion of American musical folkways. It is an excellent document of the life and work of a blues musician.

2: It would also fit in very well with a program that included such films as *Factory* and *The Young Uns*. All three are documentary films, but each has a distinctive style. In each film the film maker has chosen an aspect of his subject's existence to emphasize. It would make an interesting and profitable discussion to analyze how the film maker in each case has made clear his particular emphasis, and also how he has used the soundtrack in his film. What do we hear in each film? What don't we hear? How is the film photographed? What response does the photograph of a particular object evoke in us? There is no real need to go into these questions with a deep technical knowledge of photography or film making. Just a well organized discussion of honest reactions to the film would be most profitable.

THE SIXTIES

This film was born into the middle of a small tempest. It was originally commissioned by the Columbia Broadcasting System to be shown on their news show *Sixty Minutes*. It was cancelled at the last minute by the producer who claimed to have found it simply not good enough to be aired. There were others who thought the real reason for its last minute cancellation was due the fact that it might prove to be too controversial.

The result was that the film maker, Charles Braverman, who also made *American Time Capsule,* bought back the rights to the film so that it could be shown elsewhere, most notably at the Ann Arbor Film Festival and on NET.

The Sixties is a collage film, that is, it is a cleverly composed film that is made up of old news footage of noteworthy

events that took place during the past decade. The skill of the
film maker is brought out, or not brought out, if you happen to
be a producer at CBS, by the way the film maker puts his raw
material together. Everything from the brutality at Selma and
The Beatles' first press conference in the United States to the
Democratic National Convention in 1968 is tossed into this salad
that proved to be too hotly spiced for some tastes.

      The film is well worth viewing whether or not
we agree with its point of view. Its exploration into the depth
and variety of the American experience in the last ten years is
clever, controversial, and, above all, interesting.

14 minutes—color
Rental—$15.00 (#16)
Purchase—$175.00 (#16)

Suggestions for the Use of
THE SIXTIES

**1: This film would fit very well into any discussion
of current events in the American scene. It could serve as an
introduction to a discussion of present American experience. The
film has a very definite point of view, which is probably the
main reason it was not originally shown on television. It should be
remembered, however, that one need not totally accept that point**

of view to enjoy the film or be stimulated by it. The point is that the film makes a statement, and the audience will almost surely react to it.

2: The technique of the film is also an interesting starting point for a discussion. By technique here I mean the method the film maker uses to state his point of view. He has chosen definite shots to show us and has excluded others. How does he get across his point of view? What is the effect of having one particular shot follow another? All these questions would be fruitful if applied to an examination of this film.

THE AUTOMOBILE:
AN UNSURPASSED CONVENIENCE?
Two thirds of the land encompassed by the city of Los Angeles is covered by freeways and roads and streets and parking lots and gasoline stations and automobile salesrooms and private garages and other appurtenances of automobiling. Fumes from automobile exhaust pipes have turned the skies above the city a weird shade of yellowish green, obscuring the nearby purple-mountained majesty. On many days of every year the accumulated smog is so unbearable that school children are not allowed to play outdoors. Last year someone placed a hand-lettered sign at the city limits reading: BREATHING IS UNHEALTHY FOR CHILDREN AND OTHER GROWING THINGS. Emphysema, a lung disease caused by gases and other particulates in the air, has killed 12% more people every year for the past twenty years. The death toll from crashing automobiles is staggering. The city grows relentlessly noisier, dirtier, and uglier.
Why is this affront to public decency tolerated?
According to advertisements written and distributed at considerable expense by automobile makers, gasoline salesmen, and road builders, it is because the private automobile is an unsurpassed convenience for all of us—because it takes us wherever we need or want to go more quickly than we could get there by any other means of transportation, and in the most pleasing fashion imaginable.
Denis Hayes

THE ABANDONED

This film is a short lyrical look at the mountains of junked automobiles that our consumer economy is constantly producing. Rusted hulks of automobiles are piled endlessly on top of each other to the background accompaniment of electronic music. *The Abandoned* does not make any attempt to analyze the reasons that caused the erection of these shrines to unbridled consumerism. It simply presents us with the bare physical reality of the situation.

The Abandoned is a well made and meaningful film. It is not one, however, that would lead to a good discussion in and of itself. Ideally, it could be shown as part of an awareness seminar on ecology. It is much more of a mood film than anything else, but it is an excellent device with which to point up the raw physical ugliness that is too often a by-product of our contemporary society.

10 minutes—color
Rental—$10.00 (#12)
Purchase—$130.00 (#12)

Suggestions for the Use of
THE ABANDONED

1: The film would be best employed as part of a

program that also used slides, tape recordings, and other films. For example, it would fit in very well with other films about modern American life such as *Factory* and *The Sixties*.

2: As a simple exercise in the power of films to evoke contrasting moods, *The Abandoned* would go very well with *Starlight*. Here the discussion would most profitably center around how a film means rather than strictly what it means. Both films create a very definite atmosphere rather than a strictly definable meaning. Descriptions of what these atmospheres are and how the film maker created them in each case would make for an interesting discussion.

A PASSING PHASE

This film is a rather satiric comment on the inevitability of human progress. It is a short animated treatment of the process of evolution culminating in the growth of mankind. We first see the overview as huge fiery explosions are followed by the formation of hot masses of material, one of which eventually becomes earth. Then we see the microcosm as the chemical reactions of attractions and repulsion are pictured as small lines and x's that interact with each other.

Man then comes on the scene, a hairy brute who takes what he wants by force. He is seen killing and eating whatever he can, plants, animals, and even other men. Finally, with the progress of civilization he becomes a sophisticated killer with a splendid array of complicated but highly effective weaponry. Man's basic nature hasn't changed, though, and keeping to his unswerving pattern of destruction he ultimately manages to reverse the process of evolution and return the earth to a state of molten energy with his scientifically progressive use of nuclear energy.

A Passing Phase is short, entertaining, and to the point. When discussed in the context of a theme of happiness, it ought to provide the basis for a number of interesting questions. It is one point of view about the nature of man and, ironically, his capacity for happiness.

7 minutes—color
Rental—$15.00 (#11)
Purchase—$150.00 (#11)

Suggestions for the Use of
A PASSING PHASE

1: Have each member of the audience, or groups selected from the audience, make a short montage of photographs that parallel the development and point of the film. A montage is a series of still photographs that when viewed in sequence tell a story.

2: Discuss the point of the film in relation to the previous quote from Isaac Asimov. Is the film making the same point as Asimov? What in the film supports his position? What does not agree with Asimov?

GLASS

Glass has become recognized as a minor classic among contemporary short films. Beautiful to watch with a precision of artistic control, that becomes clearer with each viewing, the film is one that simply should not be missed. The subject of the film is the manufacture of glass, and it is a tribute to the film maker, Bert Haanstra, that he is able to invest what appears to be such a commonplace subject with such beauty and imagination. The subject he explores in the film is the dramatic difference between the modern, assembly line manufacture of glass and the lyrical skill of the traditional glassblowers.

The film does not simply present the process it depicts but somehow manages to go beyond the level of physical activity into the creative act itself. We are fascinated by the poetic movement of the artisans we see at work in the film and are caught up in the intensity of their activity.

Glass demonstrates a control of film editing that rarely has been matched. Each shot flows into the next with an eye to visual form and intellectual meaning with a rhythm that is captivating.

11 minutes—color
Rental—$20.00 (#16)

Suggestions for the Use of
GLASS

1: This film is one of the most universal in this book. The level of its artistic achievement is so high that it is worth screening for itself. The film technique the film maker uses, the shots he has selected to show us and how he puts them together, would be extremely profitable for a group interested in the art of film making.

2: *Glass* would be an outstanding film to show in a seminar attempting to deal with the theme of creativity. The creative act of the film itself and the dedication of the artisans we see in the film provide a plethora of material for discussion. *Glass* would also fit in very well with *The Searching Eye* and *Why Man Creates* in such a study. A strong visual and psychological contrast would strongly be brought out if *Glass* were shown with *Factory*. The two films deal with men in the process of manufacturing but from totally different points of view.

AN INTERVIEW WITH E. B. WHITE
You said you often went to zoos rather than write. Can you say something of discipline and the writer?
White: There are two faces to discipline. If a man (who writes) feels like going to a zoo, he should by all means go to a zoo. He might even be lucky, as I once was when I paid a call at the Bronx Zoo and found myself attending the birth

143

*of twin fawns. It was a fine sight, and I lost no time writing
a piece about it. The other face of discipline is that, zoo or no
zoo, diversion or no diversion, in the end a man must sit down
and get the words on paper, and against great odds. This
takes stamina and resolution. Having got them on paper, he
must still have the discipline to discard them if they fail to measure
up; he must view them with a jaundiced eye and do the whole
thing over as many times as are necessary to achieve excellence
(or as close to excellence as he can get). This varies from one
time to maybe twenty.*
E. B. White

A

This is an animated short from Poland. Like most of
the shorts from Eastern Europe it has a strong undercurrent of
frustration and even terror. The premise of the film is a
comically absurd one, but once it is granted by the audience, the
rest of the film follows with rigorous dramatic logic.

A man is alone in his dull ordinary flat. Suddenly,
the form of the letter "A" appears in his room, an unwelcome
intruder into his privacy. At first, the man tries patiently to
remove the letter from his room. When his initial efforts have
met with no success, he becomes more violent in his efforts. The
letter still remains present despite all his efforts to remove it.
Finally, the man is exhausted and surrenders to the domination
of the "A."

Now the action of the film takes a complete reversal.
The letter begins to attack him, pounding him and hurling him
about the room. Our hero now lies motionless utterly defeated by
the intruder. The film ends with an ironic and rather frightening
twist.

The premise of the film, while physically absurd, is
psychologically valid and hence emotionally gripping to a point
that is frightening. It is strongly reminiscent of a dream in its
imagery and development. It is this psychological validity of the
film that should make for an interesting discussion.

10 minutes—B&W
Rental—$10.00 (#6)

144

Suggestions for the Use of
A

1: Why the film affects us is perhaps the most important question a screening of *A* would suggest. The film maker has somehow struck a chord in our psyches that we respond to. If this is not the case with a particular audience, the question of why the film does not work would almost be an equally interesting question to develop.

2: *A* would fit well into a program of animated films. A comparison of its technique with such films as *Scabies*, *Acceleration* or *Sisyphus* would be an excellent base for a mini-film seminar.

ISHI IN TWO WORLDS

The Yahi Indians of California were nearly exterminated by the rapid incursions of the white man into California. Unlike the other American Indian tribes, who managed to come to some sort of arrangement for their own survival with their conquerors, a lone Yahi Indian, Yahi, was left to cope with the white man's world.

Ishi's transition from his tribal Indian life to the white world was not a gradual one. He literally stepped from one into the other. From a pastoral existence of deer hunting, berry picking, and fishing he was swept up into the life of double breasted suits and automobiles.

Ishi in Two Worlds tries to recapture the experience of Ishi's transition from one world into the other. Using still photographs and motion picture footage of the time, the film brings us the unique personality of Ishi and the qualities of the man that remained despite his cultural dislocation.

The film is a sensitive anthropological study of the far ranging implications of the clash of cultures, an element in our world which is fast becoming recognized as a vital one. What it means to be one of "them" rather than one of us is a question we must face for our own survival.

19 minutes—color & B&W
Rental—$20.00 (#6)
Purchase—$200.00 (#6)

Suggestions for the Use of
ISHI IN TWO WORLDS

1: The film's most obvious use would be for some background material in a discussion of the question of the situation of the American Indian. *The Ballad of the Crowfoot* and *Between Two Rivers* would also be of prime importance here.

2: There is a larger subject that is also treated, at least in one aspect, in the film, the question of the clash of cultures. As our modern world grows smaller and human beings are forced to deal more intimately with each other, the questions of different cultures with their almost totally divergent value systems and consequent methods of activity grow in importance. *Ishi in Two Worlds* could be used not just as the story of one man or one people, but as an introduction into the nature of the growing pains, or more precisely, the meeting pains of two cultures. *I'm a Man* deals with this critical question but from another point of view. The juxtaposition of these films should provide vital insights into this subtle but important question.

THE WHITE MAN: INDIAN VIEWS
The whites told only one side. Told it to please themselves. Told much that is not true. Only his own best deeds, only the worst deeds of the Indians, has the white man told.
Yellow Wolf of the Nez Perce

The earth was created by the assistance of the sun,
and it should be left as it was . . . The country was made
without lines of demarcation, and it is no man's business to
divide it . . . I see the whites all over the country gaining wealth,
and see their desire to give us lands which are worthless . . .
The earth and myself are of one mind. The measure of the land
and the measure of our bodies are the same. Say to us if you can
say it, that you were sent by the Creative Power to talk to us.
Perhaps you think the Creator sent you here to dispose of us as
you see fit. If you thought you were sent by the Creator I might
be induced to think you had a right to dispose of me. Do
not misunderstand me, but understand me fully with reference
to my affection for the land. I never said the land was mine
to do with it as I chose. The one who has the right to dispose of
it is the one who has created it. I claim a right to live on my
land, and accord you the privilege to live on yours.
Heinmot Tooyalaket (Chief Joseph) of the Nez Perce

ACTUA-TILT

A delightful little fantasy, which wryly comments
on the mechanization of our contemporary society, *Actua-Tilt*
makes for an excellent change of pace. The comic force of the
film flows from the use of exaggeration in developing its

premise. A simple game on a pinball machine is pushed to a fantastic but psychologically valid conclusion. *Actua-Tilt* will keep an audience enthralled for its entire 12 minutes.

12 minutes—B&W
Rental—$15.00 (#16)
Purchase—$120.00 (#16)

Suggestions for the Use of
ACTUA-TILT

1: *Actua-Tilt* **can be used by itself as an interesting probe of our human fascination with noise and light. The pinball machine is an excellent example of pandering to our pleasure at flashing lights and ringing bells. It also gets into the question of violence, and why it is such a recurring theme in our society.**

2: The film can also be used with such films as *Sales Training: Japanese Style* **and** *Comput-Her Baby* **which have a similar flashy tone. It could also be contrasted with** *Awareness***, which springs from a totally different consciousness.**

DREAM OF THE WILD HORSES

A classic of motion and form, *Dream of the Wild Horses* is a hauntingly beautiful film that cannot fail to fascinate an audience. It is a brief lyrical paean that celebrates the raw beauty of animal motion. The film is a minor masterpiece of the perfect blending of visual rhythms.

The subject of *Dream of the Wild Horses* is the motion of the wild horses of Camargue, an island in the delta of the Rhone. The experience of the film, though, seems to be taking place outside of any reference to space or time. We seem to be in another strange world as we watch the film unfold on the screen. The soundtrack, a fascinating score of electronic music, perfectly supports the mood of surreal beauty.

The film does not lead to a discussion of social problems and solutions. It is meant to be viewed, rather, as a simple poetic statement, an experience to be valued in itself. It can also be seen several times and still reveal aspects of form and motion that were not perceived in its first screening.

148

9 minutes—color
Rental—$15.00 (#6)

Suggestions for the Use of
DREAM OF THE WILD HORSES

1: *Dream of the Wild Horses* **is one of those films that stretches the limits of the creative possibilities of the film medium. Made in 1962, it still is an original and fresh experiment in how to communicate with film. It would fit in very well with** *Awareness,* **which deals more literally with the significance of the contemplation of beauty. If shown with** *Factory* **and** *The Anderson Platoon,* **it would provide an excellent contrast in both content and form and underline the radically different ways a film can communicate.**

2: *Dream of the Wild Horses* **can be shown by itself and provide the stimulus for provocative discussions on poetic form. What are the elements that make up the film? What shots does the film maker give us? In what order does he put them together? What is the importance of the slow motion in the film? How long does he allow one shot to remain on the screen in comparison to others? How does the film maker combine long shots with medium shots, close-ups? What does the soundtrack contribute to the film? Test this by screening the film silently.**

There is no need to hesitate because of a lack of technical knowledge of film making to discuss these questions. Most of these elements of the film can be perceived simply by screening the film a few times and carefully observing its makeup.

Appendix I

SOME SUGGESTIONS FOR A SUPER-8 FILM MAKING COURSE

The main requirement here for the teacher is not technical knowledge but a willingness to learn with the students. The most important ingredient for success is simply a desire to explore this interesting medium.

I: PREPARATION

The first step would be to purchase a short book from the local camera shop, *How to Make Good Home Movies*, put out by Eastman Kodak. This book is specifically designed for the beginner. It immediately puts the reader at his ease with a simple and straightforward explanation of everything from the simplest mechanics of the camera to some interesting techniques for making films with an almost professional polish.

It would also be a good idea to find a trustworthy camera dealer with whom you can do business.

151

II: EQUIPMENT

I strongly suspect that the large bulk of sales of Super-8 movie equipment are to people who use their new toys only once. As a result your best initial source of Super-8 equipment might be these stored away cameras and projectors. The main rule here is to keep the equipment simple. There is no need to spend all the extra money on sound equipped cameras or other expensive do-dads.

There are three basic pieces of equipment that you will need, a camera, a projector, and a viewer or film editor.

THE CAMERA

Super-8 is the term used to designate the size of the film which is currently the most popular for home movies. It is called Super-8 because, although it has the same dimensions as regular 8 millimeter film, it has more picture space on each frame of film. It is important to note that 8 mm. and Super-8 are *not* interchangeable in cameras or projectors unless this equipment is specifically marked as being able to handle both. As a general rule projectors and viewers can handle both gauges with a flick of a switch, cameras cannot.

Don't buy an expensive camera at first. Buy a low priced model of the Kodak line or perhaps a Bauer, a German make. All you need at first is a simple battery driven camera. If you can afford one with an adjustable focus, buy it, but avoid zoom lenses and other frills until later. This simple camera will provide 90% of the possibilities of the more expensive cameras. If treated with care, it will last through numerous assignments. As you become more expert, the more expensive cameras can be explored at your own risk.

THE PROJECTOR

This should be your major initial investment. What you are looking for here is durability, the ability to project film after film with only an occasional bulb change. Avoid the cheaper models here, if you are buying and not just borrowing one. I would advise investing from $150.00 to $250.00 retail for a projector, despite the fact that you might see specials for $50.00 to $75.00. These models are sold with the hope that the buyer will discover another hobby after screening two or three films.

Deal with a retailer you can trust and let him know it is for classroom use. Also make sure to get a warranty on the equipment and an easy method of getting the equipment repaired.

152

FILM

Super-8 film comes in cassettes that simply fit into the camera without your fingers ever having to touch the film. There are only two brands that I would recommend for their quality, Kodak and AGFA. You will see advertised bargains for cheaper film and processing, which in the long run are best to avoid. The film should come with a prepaid mailer. The dealer is important here. He might give you a break on a bulk purchase of film and let you know the best method for getting it back to you after processing.

EDITING VIEWER

This device is basically a light box with two handles for winding and rewinding the film. They normally sell for between $20.00 and $30.00. I would recommend the Vernon Dual 8 viewer. It is sturdy and provides a fairly bright picture.

The cutting of the film is done with a small guillotine splicing block which can be purchased at the local camera shop. Try and get one with metal prongs to hold the film. Some cheap models are made with plastic prongs, and the film tends to slip out of position and cause messy splices.

The film is spliced together with mylar splicing tape, which covers the frame on both sides of the splice. These come in small packets and resemble small Band-Aids.

III: TESTING THE EQUIPMENT

Before embarking on any major projects involving casts of thousands, it is a good idea to shoot a few rolls of film with the class under varying conditions. The common mistakes of beginning cinematographers will soon become evident and later avoided.

    a. shoot some film outdoors in the sun, then in the shadows

    b. shoot some close-ups (3 to 7 feet), some medium shots (7 to 15 feet) and some long shots (15 feet to infinity)

    c. pan the camera, i.e., keep it on a horizontal plane but move it from left to right

After you have shot two or three rolls, get them processed and screen them with the class as soon as possible. The most common mistake you will find is that the camera was not held steady and that the panning shots were done too quickly. Have the class comment on the various shots, and they will learn quickly what is and is not effective camera technique.

153

IV: SCRIPTING

Keep this simple at least in the beginning. A good idea is to make a story board, a comic-book-like strip with stick figures, to outline the continuity of the film. Some ideas for a short film would be:

1: Film a theme—love, hate, alienation, greed, gluttony, repression. Have the film makers pick one of these and select visuals to illustrate it. Back up or support the theme by music or narration on a tape recorder. A rough synchronization of sound and picture can be achieved with a tape recorder, but it is only approximate.

2: Do a picturetrack—Pick a pop song and make a film of the visual images it suggests to you. This usually always works.

3: A Day in the Life film—Take the material for the film from the everyday occurrences of a day in the life of a student or teacher and satirize them filmically.

4: Do a Horror Film or a Chase Film—Sometimes just by assigning a film with a title like *The Rancid Vetch, The Creeping Horror that Stalks the Bronx* a film masterpiece will result.

The important learning experience here occurs when the uncut film that has been shot is projected for the class. Mistakes that have been made will be evident and can be reshot later. One student will learn a lot from seeing the efforts of his classmates.

V: SHOOTING

At first the students should be supervised as closely as possible. They should try to know what they are about at every moment. Why are they shooting this particular shot? Is it what they planned? If not, do they think it is better? As I mentioned above these first efforts should be screened in class. A lot of missing shots will be discovered and different techniques can be compared.

After the first shooting efforts of the class have been shown, a lot of revising can be done. Some will have to be shot over, others will want to start on a more suitable project. It is important to decide this at this stage.

VI: EDITING

This is the part of the project that demands the most effort and concentration. It is a boring task compared to

154

shooting, but it usually makes the difference between a sloppy film and a polished one.

A good first rule is to label everything. All rolls of film look exactly alike and are easily lost. Label them immediately with masking tape and a magic marker.

There are three basic steps which will make editing easier.

1: View all the shots in the viewer before doing any cutting of the film. List them numerically in a notebook or on cards with a short description of each.

2: Cut the film into its shots identifying each shot with a piece of masking tape and its matching number in the notebook. You should now be able to identify any shot you have cut by a quick glance at its number on the tape and in the notebook. The film strips or cuts should be hung together in order and in one place.

3: Rearrange the shots in your notebook or on the cards. This can be done by writing a second number within a circle next to the original one. The result should be that you will know that shot number 5 is shot number 17 in the final film.

A word of caution here. Don't cut the shots for the film too closely the first time. Make them longer than you want them to be in the final film. The first thing to do is to have a *string out* or a sequence of shots in the rough order and length that you want them. After you project this a few times, you will get a better sense of the basic visual rhythm that you want to achieve. Then you can make a finer cut.

These then, are the basic elements that go into a film production course. The important thing is patience. The project will stumble along at first but then pick up momentum as it progresses. Teaching such courses has never failed to help the teacher see unsuspected dimensions in his students and himself.

Appendix II

LIST OF FILM DISTRIBUTORS

The best way to make use of this list would be to write to each of the following companies asking for their catalogs and any other information they might provide along with their films. Many of the films listed in this book are distributed by a number of distributors. It would be a good idea to check as many catalogs as possible for a particular film because, in some instances, the prices vary.

Besides the distribution companies, many large cities have fairly comprehensive film libraries as do many major universities. Check what is available in your area and the lending policies of each.

156

The American Film Institute
1815 H Street NW
Washington, D.C. 20006
The AFI is not primarily a film distributor but rather
an invaluable source of information on current developments in
film education. They have an educational membership that provides its subscribers with a regular newsletter that is well worth
the minimal dues requirement. The AFI also periodically sponsors
Film Institutes and Screenings that are of interest to film edu-
cators as well as those teachers who simply want to employ films
gainfully in classroom situations.

Association Films
Paulist Productions
17575 Pacific Coast Highway
Pacific Palisades, California 90272
This company has a number of offices around the
country for the distribution of their films. You can receive their
catalog from the above address. Association Films primarily
produces TV style short dramas geared to provoke discussion
about personal or social moral problems. They are all about
28 minutes long and come with a prepared discussion sheet
for the film.

Contemporary/McGraw-Hill Films
(Eastern Office)
Princeton Road
Hightstown, New Jersey 08520

(Midwest Office)
828 Custer Ave.
Evanston, Illinois 60202

(Western Office)
1714 Stockton St.
San Francisco, California 94133
Contemporary/McGraw-Hill might well be the largest
producer and distributor of 16 mm. films in the world. Their
catalog is an invaluable tool for anyone interested in using films.

Mass Media Ministries
2116 North Charles St.
Baltimore, Maryland 21218
or
1720 Chouteau Ave.
St. Louis, Missouri 63103

This is a fairly new and growing company which provides a number of valuable services for the film teacher. They are also involved in other media and their use in the classroom. Besides their catalog they publish a comprehensive newsletter which is an excellent source of information on new developments in the media.

NBC Educational Enterprises
Room 1040
30 Rockefeller Plaza
New York, N.Y. 10020

A few years ago NBC News decided to distribute there own news documentaries. NBC Educational Enterprises was created for that purpose. They specialize in the sale and rental of the photo-journalism films of NBC News, which are excellently done treatments of current social and political issues. NBC Educational Enterprises provides a catalog of their current releases which is kept up-to-date with a weekly supplement as well as information on upcoming NBC specials and documentaries.

Pyramid Films
Box 1048
Santa Monica, California 90406

Pyramid Films has a large collection of new and exciting experiments in 16 mm. films. There is, for example, a whole series devoted to the visual beauty of man at play. Teachers should take advantage of their comprehensive film listings and the ample printed information they provide on their films.

OTHER FILM DISTRIBUTORS

Carousel Films, Inc.
1501 Broadway
New York, N.Y. 10036

Churchill Films
662 North Robertson Blvd.
Los Angeles, California 90069

Columbia Cinematheque
711 Fifth Ave.
New York, N.Y. 10022

Encyclopedia Britannica
Educational Corporation
425 N. Michigan Ave.
Chicago, Illinois 60611

Films Inc.
1144 Wilmette Ave.
Wilmette, Illinois 60091

Graphics Curriculum, Inc.
P.O. Box 565
New York, N.Y. 10021

Grove Press, Inc.
Film Division
53 East 11th St.
New York, N.Y. 10003

International Film Bureau, Inc.
332 South Michigan Ave.
Chicago, Illinois

National Film Board of Canada
680 Fifth Ave.
New York, N.Y. 10019

New York University Film Library
26 Washington Place
New York, N.Y. 10003

Perennial Education, Inc.
1825 Willow Road
Northfield, Illinois 60093

ROA's Films
1696 North Astor St.
Milwaukee, Wisconsin 53202

Time-Life Films
43 West 16th St.
New York, N.Y. 10011

Walter Reade-Sterling Films
Educational Films, Inc.
241 East 34th St.
New York, N.Y. 10016

INDEX OF FILMS

161

9810